becoming
yourself

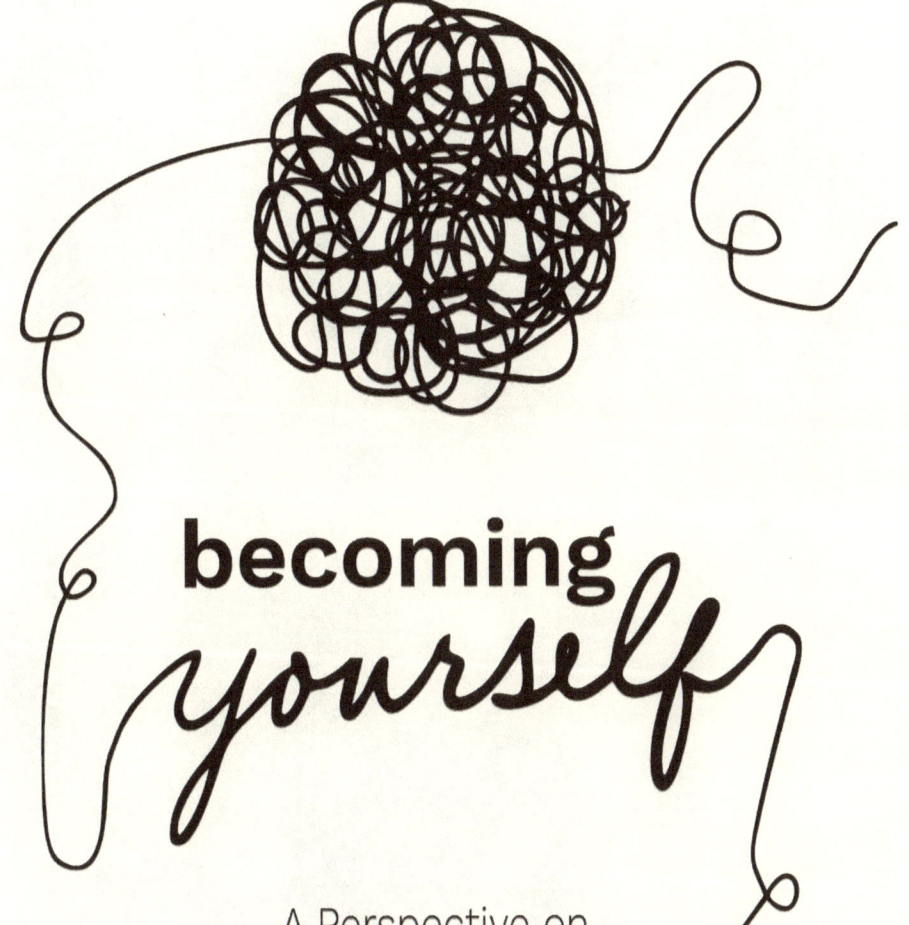

becoming
yourself

A Perspective on
Christian Character

JACK HOEY JR.

Dedication

For Mary Jane Hoey,
my mom,
whose life exemplifies
faith expressing itself through love.

becoming *yourself*
A Perspective on Christian Character

To contact the publisher, Gravitas Press, visit GravitasPress.com

To contact the author, visit www.JackHoey.com

ISBN: 979-8-9878224-8-7

Content coach: Bonnie Budzowski
Cover design: Jennifer Freemon
Interior design: Melissa Farr, Back Porch Creative LLC
Author photographer: Caroline Brogdon of Caroline Grace Photography LLC

GRAVITAS PRESS

Contents

part one

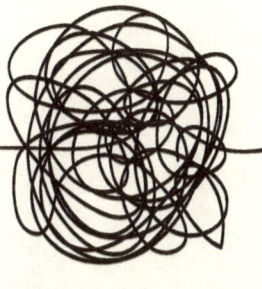

Understanding Character

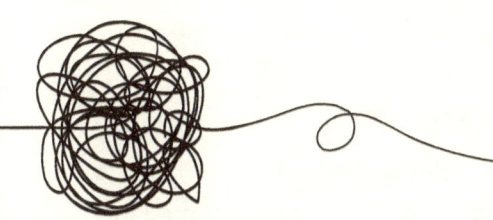

chapter one

Introduction: The Person Behind the Mask

As I sat down, I felt my phone vibrate. I was with my family at a restaurant with a long-time friend whom we hadn't seen for years. Normally, I would have ignored the call, but I saw it was my sister Susy, who rarely calls me. I answered the call and heard Susy sobbing. She was calling from the hospital; our dad had suddenly and unexpectedly died. My mind felt disconnected from my body as this paralyzing, overwhelming realization crowded out everything else. My dad was gone. I made my apologies, went home, got a few clothes, and drove to my parents' home in Hilton Head, South Carolina, just a few hours away from my home in Charleston.

My father lived a full life for eighty-five years, then passed in a moment, more than ten years ago now. As I drove to Hilton Head that night, I began a process of reflection, repeated multiple times in the months that followed, on my father's life and the legacy he left for me.

Like many boys, I idolized my dad. As a child, I had an unreflecting acceptance of my parents' world; it didn't occur to me that things could be different from how they were. As I matured, I came to realize that my parents' lives and the home they made for me and my five siblings were produced by choices they made, and I realized that my parents' choices were exceptionally wise.

Dad exuded a quiet strength, tempered by kindness and consideration for others. He achieved great successes, but he never acted as if he were better than anyone else. Dad knew every person by name in the large headquarters office where he worked as an executive for most of his career. He enjoyed good things but sacrificed his own desires to provide for his family year after year. Even after their six children were grown and gone, Dad and Mom regularly invested in bringing their children and their large brood of grandchildren together.

Over the years, people have often told me that they see much of my father in me. I understand why. Because I admired Dad, I observed closely how he did things. I modeled many of my life patterns after his, creating numerous points of resemblance between us. But these surface similarities, at least early on, masked an important underlying difference.

As a young man, I thought I could simply adopt the traits my father exemplified as I might put on a jacket. I thought that becoming a good person meant developing a certain kind of persona. For example, I admired the settled calmness I saw in my dad. He rarely became angry, and I don't recall ever seeing him really flustered by difficult situations or events.

In contrast to Dad's equanimity, even under stress, I carried a great deal of tension as a young man, which often found release in explosions of anger. I didn't enjoy living with a churning stomach, and I hated the impact my anger sometimes had on others. But my attempts to manifest the calmness I saw in my father only magnified the stress I felt.

Eventually, I came to realize that my father was calm *within himself.* He wasn't masking fear, worry, or anger. His outward calm reflected a genuinely untroubled spirit. Those qualities of my father that I most wanted to possess were ones that I needed to *embody.* They were not an outward covering; instead, they flowed from the inside out. In effect,

I had been trying to disguise myself, when I actually needed to change myself.

This recognition was a turning point in my life. In Romans 12:2, Paul exhorts each of us to "be transformed by the renewal of your mind." This is the process I began at my turning point, a process that continues to this day.

There is a memorable line in a journal entry by Søren Kierkegaard, the Danish philosopher, written shortly after his conversion experience. Musing on what the outworking of his new faith will mean for his life, he ends with these words: "Now, with God's help, I shall become myself."[1]

As we'll see, developing Christian character entails more than adhering to rules and behaving with morality. It's more complicated and more interesting than that. We are God's handiwork, and he has made each of us just as he wanted us to be. As we grow in our relationship with Christ, we grow into the selves he designed us to be even as we become more like Christ. Growing in godliness is a rich and challenging journey of coming to know God more intimately as we come to appreciate our personal design and purpose in this life. To use Paul's word, this is transformative. It's the process of becoming ourselves in Christ.

I invite you to walk with me as we explore what it means to embody the qualities of Christian character.

My dad's character reflected his lifelong pursuit of Jesus Christ. In the years since he died, reflecting on his life and on our relationship has enabled me to better understand my own struggle to live a life transformed by Christ.

I'm convinced of the importance of this struggle, because we live amid evil and brokenness. Our world brims over with selfishness, hostility, and deceit. On any given day, the news leaves me shaking my head as it depicts incompetence, indifference, and even corruption in our government, businesses, and schools, along with the malice that poisons relationships between people and nations. And many ministries, though operating with the best of intentions, accomplish little to address the problems they were formed to solve.

A quote often attributed to the Russian writer Tolstoy expresses the crux of society this way: "Everyone thinks of changing the world, but no one thinks of changing himself."

Our world disappoints us because it is filled with flawed people. As I've just acknowledged, I am one of those flawed people. So are you. Every day, our actions and words frustrate, wound, or aggravate those around us. Even the best of us often betray the standards of behavior we should reasonably expect from ourselves and from one another. The truth is that we are what is wrong with the world.

If we want to see a change in the world, we must begin with ourselves. Paul the Apostle exhorts us: "Be very careful, then, how you live—not as unwise but as wise, making the most of every opportunity, because the days are evil" (Eph. 5:15–16). This, paradoxically, is good news; the evil of our times is not a reason for despair. Rather, life presents us with an opportunity. As God fulfills his will through the progress of history, we are offered the gift of participating in his work.

It's humbling to reflect seriously on what it means to change ourselves, and it can feel overwhelming—until we recognize that changing ourselves is not a task we are asked to perform on our own. The task is monumental, but if you've called upon Jesus as your savior, the work is already begun. Furthermore, God has promised to carry on the good work he began in you and me until its completion on the day of Christ (Phil. 1:6). I am encouraged and energized in my quest to grow in godly character, because I can see that God is at work in me. There are days and seasons when this work is hard to see, but I can persevere even at those times by remembering the truth that God is the one transforming me.

Because of my own flaws, I have some trepidation about sharing with you what I have learned and am learning. I write as a fellow traveler, nothing more. My background includes experiences that will be common to many of you: married for many years, now divorced; I am a son, brother, father, and grandfather; I've been a member of a wide range of churches as I've moved around the country over the years. I've worked primarily in business settings, in companies ranging from global giants to local start-ups, but I also led a large church staff for several years. I've served in executive roles and as a consultant to both businesses and ministries. I've served in a wide range of ministries and nonprofit organizations, often as a board member, but also serving meals in a homeless shelter and teaching four-year-olds in Sunday school classrooms.

I share this range of experiences not because it means I now know everything, but because I am constantly entering new settings where I must learn how to depend on God's grace. Peter tells us, "His divine power has given us *everything we need* for life and godliness" (2 Pet. 1:3, emphasis added), but we must learn to harness the grace and power he extends to us.

For forty years, the prophet Jeremiah warned the nation of Judah that its idolatry and consistent oppression of the poor would bring about God's punishment. In the early years of his ministry, Jeremiah recorded a disturbing word from the Lord: "Go up and down the streets of Jerusalem, look around and consider, search through her squares. If you can find but one person who deals honestly and seeks the truth, I will forgive this city" (Jer. 5:1).

The Bible provides many such glimpses of the spiritual impact one person or a handful of people can have. God promised that if Abraham could find ten righteous men in Sodom and Gomorrah, the two cities would be spared from destruction (Gen. 18:20–32). He also spoke to the prophet Ezekiel, expressing his disgust with the sinfulness of Israel and its princes, saying, "I looked for a man among them who would build up the wall and stand before me in the gap on behalf of the land so I would not have to destroy it, but I found none" (Ezek. 22:30).

Because the impact of a godly life is profound, seeking to "live a life worthy of the calling you have received" (Eph. 4:1) is not merely a nice thing to do. This life choice has spiritual reverberations beyond what we can see, and at which we can only guess.

Reflect for a few moments on the night that Jesus was betrayed. He said to his disciples, "I chose you and appointed you so that you might go and bear fruit—fruit that will last" (John 15:16). This is his purpose for us—this is how we participate in his work. We honor Jesus and bring God the Father glory when we live fruitful lives: "This is to my Father's glory, that you bear much fruit, showing yourselves to be my disciples" (John 15:8).

Do you see the twist Jesus gives to the metaphor of "fruit that will last"? Fruit, as we know it, doesn't last. It's perishable and will rot every time. Jesus joins conflicting images to arrest our attention. We often equate the fruit our lives produce with the tasks we perform, but these, too, are evanescent.

In Ephesians, Paul explains that "the fruit of the light consists in all goodness, righteousness and truth" (Eph. 5:9). Fruit that *can* last is produced by the "goodness, righteousness and truth" that flow out of us. Producing this kind of fruit requires a character that embodies those things. As Jesus also explained, a tree is known by its fruit. It is not possible for a bad tree to produce good fruit, no matter how you disguise it (Matt. 7:17–18). Good fruit is produced by a tree that is good to its core and through its roots.

We don't become "good to the core" by putting on a coat or mask. We get there by cooperating with God's grace in our lives. Godly character is a daily journey, not a one-time destination. The author of Hebrews spoke of running a race, pushing forward with perseverance (Heb. 12:1). Our race involves both who we are and what we do; being and doing are tightly entwined in the pursuit of godly character.

In addition to honoring God and doing his will in the world, godly character forms the foundation for our own spiritual health and well-being. Consider the metaphor with which Jesus culminates the Sermon on the Mount.

> Everyone who hears these words of mine and puts them into practice is like a wise man who built his house on the rock. The rain came down, the streams rose, and the winds blew and beat against that house; yet it did not fall, because it had its foundation on the rock. But everyone who hears these words of mine and does not put them into practice is like a foolish man who built his house on sand. The rain came down, the streams rose, and the winds blew and beat against that house, and it fell with a great crash. (Matt. 7:24–27)

Jesus is telling us that the reason we sometimes succumb to the storms of life is that we hear his words, we may even affirm them, but we do not put them into practice. In other words, we neglect to apply Jesus' teaching in our daily lives. We don't act on it. Putting Jesus' words into practice involves action through daily attitudes, disciplines, and habits. This is how we run the race and become a good tree that bears good fruit. It's how we cooperate with God's Spirit and build an adequate spiritual foundation upon which to live.

If we fail to affirm and act on the words of Christ, at some point the rain will come down, the streams will rise, and the winds will blow and beat against us. And when the façade we have presented to the world is swept away, there will be little left standing.

Character that is worthy of our calling will equip us both to survive life's storms and to make a positive impact in our world.

Before we consider the specifics of Christian character—what it means to be good to the core—we need to further define what we mean by this term. Each of us likely has a different set of associations with the concept of Christian character. Before you begin the next chapter, take a few moments to reflect on the following questions:

- From your perspective, what is the definition of Christian character? What does this phrase mean to you?
- How do you pursue it?
- How do we make abstract concepts like goodness and righteousness practical?

Let's explore these questions and arrive at a definition we can use for our walk together.

chapter two

Foundations of Christian Character

When I think about how to define character, one image that comes to mind is Will Kane, the character played by Gary Cooper in the classic Western film *High Noon*. The movie opens in a small town on Kane's wedding day; he and his bride are about to depart and begin a new life together. Before they can leave, Kane learns that three desperadoes who terrorized the town years earlier have been released from prison and are heading toward the town for their revenge.

Kane has every right to leave as planned. He has retired as the sheriff, and the town is no longer his responsibility—but he stays to protect the people he has long served. Ironically, as he tries to rally support, the townspeople, for whom he is choosing to risk his life, refuse to help. As the film reaches its climax, Kane faces the arriving gunmen alone.

For me, that's a noble picture. Will Kane commits himself to ideals more important than his own plans and desires—more important even than his life.

This picture may produce different feelings for you. There is ambiguity in the way Kane is depicted. For example, he is willing to risk his new wife's happiness for his code of honor. Sharpening this point of conflict, his wife is a Quaker and committed to nonviolence. Like her, some may take issue with Kane's willingness to kill to protect. Furthermore, the townspeople that Kane seeks to protect are a smarmy group, thoroughly unworthy of protection. There are shadows in the picture of Will Kane; it is not all sunshine. Whatever your view of Kane's values and choices, he is walking a path of integrity, choosing to live consistently with his highest values, even if it costs him his life. It's hard to imagine a higher test of character.

As this example shows, the test of character is rarely as simple as choosing between shining goodness and unadulterated evil. That's not really a test, is it? Real tests of character involve ambiguity. Not only do we usually operate with incomplete information, but aspects of good and evil are embodied in each alternative.

Let me offer this definition of character: *your character embodies your capacity to live well.* Good character is not only grounded in wise principles and sound values, but also builds upon this foundation, so that these principles and values are expressed consistently through behavior.

Your character comprises the resources you possess for responding to life's challenges and opportunities. It's far more complicated than modeling certain behaviors or following a set of rules. The Pharisees were meticulous at following rules, but Jesus called them a brood of vipers (see Matt. 3:7).

Good character requires an insight into life that goes beyond learning lessons and rules, enabling us to be discerning and wise as we apply what we know and believe. When we have everyday opportunities to be helpful to our neighbors, co-workers, and friends, and even in chance encounters, we can choose to act with love and consideration. But character is particularly revealed in difficult times—when we are in danger or when we are tempted. I once heard character defined as "what comes out when we are squeezed." When under attack, defeated, or even ruined, good character enables us to persevere.

Describing character as a set of resources, or as a response to circumstances, may seem like an indirect approach. Rather than stating plainly what character is, I am attempting to describe what it looks like. That's how we experience character in others. Doctors, accountants, and welders can be identified by the credentials they have acquired. We recognize character, though, by how we experience a person.

Compared to other cultures and other times, our culture doesn't consider good character an important pursuit. In part, this is because we don't acknowledge the moral complexity of decision-making. First, our society has elevated self-fulfillment to an absolute good, along with its cousin, self-expression. We admire those who chase their own desires regardless of the codes they violate. Nothing can be allowed to stand in the way of finding fulfillment. The only thing that counts is getting what you want.

This belief is justified by a second, less obvious, assumption—that people are naturally good. We desperately want to believe that, left to themselves, under normal circumstances, people will choose to be kind rather than cruel, generous rather than selfish. If this were true, it would be good and healthy to put our own desires first, since what we want is naturally good. By pairing the value of self-fulfillment with the assumption of human goodness, we get what we want, and everything turns out well in the end.

However, what the Bible teaches, and what Jesus requires of his followers, takes us in a completely different direction. Self-fulfillment is not the biblical standard for a good life. Jesus challenges us to ask ourselves, "What good is it for a man to gain the whole world, yet forfeit his soul?" (Mark 8:36). When we accept God's gift of salvation, we acknowledge that we can no longer define the terms on which we live our lives: "You are not your own; you were bought at a price" (1

Cor. 6:19–20). In contrast, when self-fulfillment is our highest pursuit, we think we are freeing ourselves, but all we achieve is the freedom to explore the limitless emptiness of life apart from God.

There is a paradox here: The freedom we expect to find in self-fulfillment traps us in an imprisoning void. Acknowledging God as our Lord opens the door to freedom from a self-fulfilling way of life that leads to death—because we are not naturally good.

Paul begins his sampling of Old Testament quotations in Romans 3 with these words: "There is no one righteous, not even one" (Rom. 3:10). He goes on to mourn that "there is no one who understands, no one who seeks God. All have turned away, they have together become worthless" (vv. 11–12).

Importantly, though, we are not to accept this situation, for it is not the end of the matter. The New Testament is filled with exhortation to live lives that express love, kindness, and goodness—qualities of character that will each be the focus of a coming chapter. I love the way James describes character: "Who is wise and understanding among you? Let him show it by his good life, by deeds done in the humility that comes from wisdom" (Jas. 3:13).

If we are not naturally good, how do we become good? In Philippians 1:6, Paul assures us that "he who began a good work in you will carry it on to completion until the day of Christ Jesus." God's Spirit infuses us with the power to produce the fruit of life—fruit that comes from the Holy Spirit rather than the desires of our sinful nature. Godly character, then, is not something we can produce on our own. John Henry Newman framed this point succinctly: "It is but building on the sand to profess to believe in Christ, yet not to acknowledge that without Him we can do nothing."[2]

Walking with God joyfully and faithfully does not automatically happen once we believe. We must cooperate with the Holy Spirit's work, developing the capacity to take hold of the grace God extends.

"Be imitators of God, therefore, as dearly loved children and live a life of love" (Eph. 5:1–2).

Paul depicts this way of life in Ephesians 4. He writes that Christ has given spiritual gifts to the church:

> . . . so that the body of Christ may be built up until we all reach unity in the faith and in the knowledge of the Son of God and become mature, attaining to the whole measure of the fullness of Christ. Then we will no longer be infants, tossed back and forth by the waves, and blown here and there by every wind of teaching and by the cunning and craftiness of men in their deceitful scheming. Instead, speaking the truth in love, we will in all things grow up into him who is the Head, that is, Christ. (Eph. 4:12–15)

We see three crucial points about godly character in this passage. First, *godly character always comes from Christ and looks like Christ.* Maturity means "attaining to the whole measure of the fullness of Christ."

We sometimes define a person with good character as someone who can be relied upon. The truth is that none of us, on our own, can be fully relied upon, because none of us fully outgrows our vulnerability to spiritual failure. We never outgrow our need for God's Spirit. Character does not give us the ability to stand on our own; we will never be more than weak, needy, deeply flawed creatures. Rather, as we will see, character is the measure of our capacity to be channels for God's grace. Said another way, developing character is not a matter of what we can do to strengthen ourselves, but of learning to take hold of the grace and power that God makes available to us. This comes as we grow into maturity and fullness in Christ.

The second point builds on the first. *We are meant to "in all things grow up into him who is the Head, that is, Christ."* The quality of a person's character is rooted in their concept of Christ as they manifest the image of God. If my concept of God is small, selfish, and mean, my ideals and aspirations will be small, selfish, and mean. The character I shape cannot be higher or better than my concept of God.

The God that the Bible shows us, and whom we are invited to experience, has an infinitely loving nature. A few verses further on, Paul admonishes us to "live a life of love, just as Christ loved us and gave himself up for us" (Eph. 5:2). This is what we must train ourselves to do through a lifetime of discipline. Character, though it is integral to a person, is not only an interior quality; it is also relational, and it is expressed by our capacity to love.

If this is so, the qualities that shape our choices and responses should be the highest and best qualities that our understanding is capable of. How do we come to know what they are and what they look like? Furthermore, how do we learn to change and grow so these qualities can be seen in us by others?

The answer is found in the third point. Paul tells us that the church has been given spiritual gifts to build us up "until we all reach unity in the faith and in the *knowledge of the Son of God*" (Eph. 4:13, emphasis added). We will examine the importance of knowledge in a later chapter. It cannot be over-emphasized. Without knowledge of Christ, our maturity will be stunted; we will be as infants, "tossed back and forth by the waves, and blown here and there by every wind of teaching and by the cunning and craftiness of men in their deceitful scheming" (Eph. 4:14).

Love, in the way we often think of it, is not enough. Love is much more than feelings. Paul tells the Philippian church that his prayer for them is "that your love may abound more and more in knowledge and depth of insight, so that you may be able to discern what is best" (Phil. 1:9–10).

Christians believe God has revealed the truths by which we should live. But those of us who have lived long enough or experienced enough of life, know that revelation comes in many different guises. How do we recognize revelation when it comes?

During my college years, I began to understand and explore my talents, and I was ambitious to develop them to the full, intent on making my mark in the world. During my senior year, I committed my life to God through Jesus Christ. It seemed to me that believing the truth was not enough; I also wanted to serve him well. If obedience was important to God, and if there were things that he wanted to accomplish through me, then training myself to do those things with excellence was valuable and important.

American culture prizes success, and we tend to think that success is a function of what a person does. Accordingly, I channeled my desire to serve God well into becoming an outstanding and accomplished *doer* in my work and other endeavors. This is what I thought it meant to be effective and productive.

Then one day, a passage from 2 Peter jumped off the page at me. I had read this passage many times before, yet in that moment I read those words in a new light.

Early one morning, almost forty years ago, I sat on the couch in the living room to read my Bible. I've always been an early riser, and with preschool-age children at home in that season, the only time I could find peace and quiet was when they were still asleep.

We were living in Boulder, Colorado; it was December, and snow blanketed the frozen ground in the predawn darkness. That year, I was using a daily plan to read through the Bible from beginning to end in one year. Having reached 2 Peter in December, I was nearing the end of both the book and the year. I quote the passage below, beginning with verses 3 and 4 to provide the context:

His divine power has given us everything we need for life and godliness through our knowledge of him who called us by his own glory and goodness. Through these he has given us his very great and precious promises, so that through them you may participate in the divine nature and escape the corruption in the world caused by evil desires. For this very reason, make every effort to add to your faith goodness; and to goodness, knowledge; and to knowledge, self-control; and to self-control, perseverance; and to perseverance, godliness; and to godliness, brotherly kindness; and to brotherly kindness, love. For if you possess these qualities in increasing measure, they will keep you from being ineffective and unproductive in your knowledge of our Lord Jesus Christ. (2 Peter 1:3-8)

That last sentence is the one that leapt from the page that morning: *"If you possess these qualities in increasing measure, they will keep you from being ineffective and unproductive in your knowledge of our Lord Jesus Christ."*

I was in my early years as a parent and a professional; I had only recently taken initial steps in ministry. I was working hard to become the effective doer that exemplified my understanding of being effective and productive.

Peter's words chopped at the root of my assumptions.

"If you possess these *qualities* in increasing measure, *they* will keep you from being ineffective and unproductive" (emphasis added). Effectiveness and fruitfulness are a function of the qualities that are expressed in and through your life. Attaining maturity in Christ is the process of coming to embody godly qualities. This is not the same as what you do. *You are effective and productive based on who you are and what flows out of you in acts of love, not on what you achieve.*

In Chapter 1, I shared my experience of trying to "put on" the character I saw in my father and what I learned in the process. Peter's message in this passage speaks to what I was struggling to understand: that any quality we wish to manifest outwardly must flow from within. If we want to manifest goodness, for example, we must become good inside. Anything else is not only unsustainable, but also false.

When I faced these truths that winter morning, the direction of my life's journey changed. Change has been gradual, more like turning a giant container ship than making a quick U-turn in my car. Slowly, I began to understand that God's will for my life was not to fill a resume with accomplishments. Instead, I fulfill God's will for my life when I "possess these qualities in increasing measure," when I come to embody faith, goodness, knowledge, self-control, perseverance, godliness, brotherly kindness, and love.

If we want meaningful lives, nothing is more important than understanding how we should live in view of life's ultimate meaning and purpose. The Bible teaches that all human history marches toward a singular fulfillment.

Everything that exists is moving toward the place and time when God will put everything under his Son. Paul expresses our common destiny in these words: "He [God] made known to us the mystery of his will according to his good pleasure, which he purposed in Christ, to be put into effect when the times will have reached their fulfillment—*to bring all things in heaven and on earth together under one head, even Christ*" (Eph. 1:9–10, emphasis added).

This is true today in the heavenly realms, where God has already "seated him [Christ] at his right hand in the heavenly realms, far above all rule and authority, power and dominion, and every title that can be given, not only in the present age but also in the one to come. And God placed all things under his feet" (Eph. 1:20–22).

As we look toward that day of fulfillment, we live in a world that is hungry for Christ.

Paul writes, "The creation waits in eager expectation for the sons of God to be revealed" (Rom. 8:19). In the meantime, creation is "groaning as in the pains of childbirth right up to the present time" (Rom. 8:22).

When what we say and do expresses the love and faith and kindness that are embodied in us, we reveal something that our world hungers for. We respond to a deep yearning in the hearts of our family, neighbors, co-workers, and the people we meet. We display Christ's character to the world.

This may sound like an ethereal, semi-mystical take on life, yet its implications are immensely practical. And as Peter points out, we can live fully in this way: "His divine power has given us everything we need for life and godliness through our knowledge of him" (2 Pet. 1:3). Our knowledge of God provides the foundation for faith. His power, active in us through the Holy Spirit, enables us to live our faith in a sometimes indifferent, sometimes hostile world that averts its eyes from its spiritual need.

How do we provide a taste of the Spirit's power to a hungry world? Peter lays down a specific path for us: "Make every effort to add to your faith goodness; and to goodness, knowledge; and to knowledge, self-control; and to self-control, perseverance; and to perseverance, godliness; and to godliness, brotherly kindness; and to brotherly kindness, love" (2 Pet. 1:5–7).

In the first part of this book, we will study each of the seven qualities Peter identifies. We'll "make every effort" to understand what they mean in the context of Scripture and how we might apply them to our lives. If we possess these qualities of character, they will enable us to be effective and productive—to bear fruit that will last. These qualities provide "everything we need for life and godliness" (2 Pet. 1:3). Everything.

Growing in these qualities is a lifelong project. Importantly, it is not a matter of great accomplishments or mountaintop experiences. Instead, it is rooted in our ordinary, everyday lives.

Recently, my son told me an anecdote about a conversation that a young American missionary had with a counterpart from a different side of the world. The young American said, "I can't help but think that God has an amazing purpose for my life."

The other man responded, "Of course you think so, you're an American."

My son thought this was hilarious, depicting as it does the way American Christians often conflate biblical teaching with our culture's distinctive worldview.

In most churches I have attended, the young American's comment would be heard approvingly. God's unique and infinitely special purpose for each of us is a staple of evangelical teaching. It would not occur to most people who have been raised in such a church that this idea is derived more from American culture than sound theology. It's very easy to ascribe universal validity to things rooted in one's own culture.

In his outstanding survey of Western thought, *Sources of the Self,* Charles Taylor describes a fundamental feature of Christian spirituality as "the affirmation of ordinary life."[3] According to the Aristotelian ethical framework that dominated thought at the beginning of the Christian era, the humdrum of day-to-day living was merely the scaffolding for those aspects of life that were truly important—"the 'good life' of contemplation and one's action as a citizen."[4] Public life was deemed significant; private life was not.

In contrast, Christianity teaches that *ordinary life*—how we treat our family members, neighbors, friends, and others—is of primary value. The good life is lived when we "live a life of love, just as Christ loved us" (Eph. 5:2), not when we achieve something in the public sphere that wins us praise. "Better a patient man than a warrior, a man who controls his temper rather than one who takes a city" (Prov. 16:32).

The Bible roots our important social roles in God's design. The Bible records God's first comment about humans: "It is not good for the man to be alone" (Gen. 2:18). The Bible contains much instruction on how we are to live as members of families and communities. These teachings have been elaborated through the centuries by people seeking to live together peaceably.

When asked, "'Teacher, which is the greatest commandment in the Law?' Jesus replied: 'Love the Lord your God with all your heart and with all your soul and with all your mind. This is the first and greatest commandment. And the second is like it: Love your neighbor as yourself. All the Law and the Prophets hang on these two commandments.'" (Matt. 22:36–40).

For followers of Christ, the end toward which we are working in our day-to-day social roles is to love God and love our neighbors. The quality of an action is determined by the extent to which it expresses this love.

And so, the process of growing in these qualities of character takes place in the context of our ordinary roles and responsibilities—at work, in our parenting, in our marriages, and in our communities.

Paul taught the Thessalonian church, "Make it your ambition to lead a quiet life" (1 Thess. 4:11). The Greek word *hēsychazō* translated as "quiet" in this verse evokes not silence but rather a rooted tranquility. It is the same word Peter uses when he advises women to seek a beauty that comes not from outward adornment but from "your inner self, the unfading beauty of a gentle and *quiet* spirit" (1 Pet. 3:4, emphasis added). We have talked about how the qualities of character must be embodied—that their outward expression must flow from an inner reality. In the same way, a quiet life is rooted in quietness of spirit.

Paul goes on to teach how this inner tranquility is to be expressed:

Make it your ambition to lead a quiet life, to mind your own business and to work with your hands, just as we told you, so that your daily life may win the respect of outsiders and so that you will not be dependent on anybody. (1 Thess. 4:11–12)

As I've sought to follow this teaching, I've identified several life disciplines, rooted in attitudes of mind and heart, that help me move in the right direction and then stay on track. These include cultivating a humble and responsive heart; learning what it means to pray without ceasing; honoring my commitments to family, friends, and church; seeking accountability; performing my work unto the Lord; and furthering justice. These are the core disciplines that make for a transformed life, a tree that bears good fruit. In Part 3 of this book, we will explore each of these disciplines and seek to find ways to integrate them into our lives.

It's a formidable list. Building Christian character demands marathon-style endurance rather than an adrenaline-fueled sprint. We progress by perseveringly taking small steps in the same direction, sustained by God's power working through us. We will fail and need to start over again—and again. The God who sustains us is patient and forgiving. As David says in Psalm 103, "he remembers that we are dust." If we are faithful in taking small steps, the Spirit of God will enable the growth.

Our path to Christian character must also incorporate the spiritual disciplines that Jews and Christians have practiced for millennia. The very first Psalm describes how meditating on God's law makes a person like a tree that yields its fruit in season. As we practice the spiritual disciplines, we place ourselves before God so that he can shape us into devoted, fruit-bearing people. Part 2 of this book addresses spiritual disciplines that help us grow in our relationship with God and become more like Christ. These include practicing solitude, engaging in prayer and Bible reading, and worshipping in community. We'll address each of these practices in separate, short chapters, recognizing that they overlap in multiple ways.

You may have noted that service is not identified as one of the central disciplines for developing and sustaining growth. Jesus came not to be served, but to serve (Matt. 20:28), and surely that should be true of us. *Serving* others is inseparable from *loving* them; serving is love expressed in action. But for this very reason, I am reluctant to create a separate category for service, which would imply a distinct kind of activity. Instead, serving others pervades all of life's activities and relationships. We will review this connection as we discuss the life disciplines and spiritual disciplines in Parts 2 and 3.

With this foundation in place, let's turn to examine each of the seven qualities, to understand what they mean and what it looks like to embody them.

chapter three

Faith

His divine power has given us everything we need for life and godliness through our knowledge of him who called us by his own glory and goodness. Through these he has given us his very great and precious promises, so that through them you may participate in the divine nature and escape the corruption in the world caused by evil desires.

For this very reason, make every effort to add to your **faith** *. . .*

2 PETER 1:3–5

Faith forms the indispensable foundation for character, because it provides the basis for living in God's presence. We have defined character as that which embodies our capacity to live well. We cannot live well apart from God's presence, or without the grace, strength, and guidance he provides.

"Without faith it is impossible to please God" (Heb. 11:6). Not *unlikely* to please God—impossible. The writer of Hebrews gives two essential qualities for this faith that pleases God. First, "anyone who comes to him must believe that he exists." That seems obvious, but we need to go beyond the believer-atheist dichotomy to fully understand this statement.

Over the centuries, human beings have thought about the divine in many ways. When the writer of Hebrews says we "must believe that he exists," he means we must believe in the existence of the one true God, the God who is revealed in the pages of Scripture and who was made manifest in the person of Jesus Christ on earth.

The Bible teaches that God is the pre-existent creator of all things and the immanent in all that exists; he is omniscient, omnipresent, and omnipotent; he is holy and good. We must believe in the God who is, not some other god of our imagination.

God is awesome and powerful beyond anything we can imagine, but he is also a person—a person who seeks a relationship with every one of us. His all-encompassing love for us is beyond our limited understanding, and his love will never fail.

Paul expresses the deathless power of God's love in these terms: "I am convinced that neither death nor life, neither angels nor demons, neither the present nor the future, nor any powers, neither height nor depth, nor anything else in all creation, will be able to separate us from the love of God that is in Christ Jesus our Lord" (Rom. 8:38–39).

In accordance with that love, the writer of Hebrews provides a second indispensable quality of the faith that pleases God: "He rewards those who earnestly seek him" (Heb. 11:6).

God is good; he loves us; and he treats us in accordance with his goodness and his love. In other words, "he rewards" not in the ways that you or I would reward—a reciprocal transaction with someone who has done us a good turn, or a bonus for a deserving employee, or as a special privilege for a maturing child. Rather, God himself is the reward for those who earnestly seek him.

"In thy presence is fulness of joy" (Ps. 16:11, KJV). As one of the early Hebrew prophets said, "If you seek him, he will be found by you"

(2 Chr. 15:2). Good gifts are part of that, but they are available because God is good, and we are connected to him. In fact, they cannot be enjoyed as good *unless* we are connected to him.

The faith described in these passages is more than an intellectual assent to the probability, or even the certainty, of God's existence. As Peter explains, through God's glory and goodness, "he has given us his very great and precious promises," and through these, we have "everything we need for life and godliness" (2 Pet. 1:3). In other words, *real faith provides both motive and means for action.*

And yet, we often experience a gap between the promise and its fulfillment. In fact, there's a sense in which this is always true—after all, a promise fulfilled is no longer in effect. But if our belief is in a good and faithful God, and this God's power is such that no obstacle can possibly thwart his ability to keep a promise, then we have the assurance that God will keep his promises. We, in turn, can live our lives in accordance with that assurance. God's promises are the anchors that keep our faith securely moored in the middle of a storm. He gave his promises so that we can live as Jesus did, filled with God's spirit and able to remain holy, pure, and uncorrupted by evil desires.

God's promises cover the cosmos, but he has also made specific promises to each of his followers. We reviewed in Chapter 2 his promise to bring everything in heaven and on earth under Christ. All of history is moving in this direction. Because we know the outcome, as Paul writes in 1 Corinthians 15:58, we can "stand firm. Let nothing move you. Always give yourselves fully to the work of the Lord, because you know that your labor in the Lord is not in vain." And yet, when we feel alone or in danger, we can remember and rely on the promise "Never will I leave you, never will I forsake you" (Heb. 13:5). Faith in God's promises is the ultimate resource for living well. As Peter expresses it, through these promises we are enabled to "participate in the divine nature and escape the corruption in the world caused by evil desires" (2 Pet. 1:4).

"Faith is being sure of what we hope for and certain of what we do not see" (Heb. 11:1). For most followers of Christ, here is where the challenge arises. Whether we meet this challenge or fail to do so is determined by our response to the tests of faith that God allows to enter our lives. None of us reaches the point where the process of testing ends, no matter how mature or how strong in the Lord we become.

Luke's gospel illustrates the test of faith with a poignant story. John the Baptist sent two of his disciples to Jesus to ask him, "Are you the one who was to come, or should we expect someone else?" (Luke 7:19).

If you know what the Bible tells us about John, this must seem like a strange question for John to ask. God revealed Jesus' identity to John at the start of Jesus' ministry. John proclaimed Jesus boldly, pointing him out to his own disciples with these words: "Look, the Lamb of God who takes away the sin of the world!" (John 1:29). He baptized Jesus at Jesus' request and saw the Holy Spirit descend on him like a dove. How, then, could John ask if Jesus was "the one"?

John asked this question from a prison cell. He had been imprisoned unjustly for, as a twenty-first-century American might say, speaking the truth to power. He admonished Herod, the king of the land, about his adulterous, unlawful marriage to Herodias, his brother Philip's wife. At her instigation, Herod put John in prison. Meanwhile, Jesus was traveling all over the country, performing miracles and demonstrating his amazing power. John likely wondered from his jail cell, *Why doesn't Jesus use his power to help me? After all, I was his mentor in ministry. Once he began teaching, I stepped into the background. I didn't have to do that. He's even my cousin! A man who can raise the dead could get me out of this prison if he wanted to. Why doesn't he?*

The Bible tells us, "A righteous man may have many troubles, but the Lord delivers him from them all" (Ps. 34:19). But John didn't see any deliverance in the human sense. Can you see how his faith might have wavered? I doubt there's been a Christ-follower in the last two thousand years who hasn't wavered in the face of suffering or loss. I say this with assurance, because God tests us to the point where we do waver. If faith isn't tested to the breaking point, then it's not really a test.

Jesus responded generously to John's disciples, saying, "I tell you, among those born of women there is no one greater than John" (Luke 7:28). But his response also contained a challenge. After pointing John's disciples to the miracles that he had performed as evidence that he was indeed "the one," Jesus then said, "Blessed is the man who does not fall away on account of me" (Luke 7:23).

Essentially, he was saying: *Yes, I am the one. And John, I know what you would naturally expect, but for reasons I am not going to share with you, I will not release you from prison. Are you still willing to believe in a Messiah who will treat you like that? Are you willing to trust me when my actions don't seem to make sense?*

God is good, but *his goodness isn't always evident in our circumstances.* In those times, we must decide what we will believe. We must decide if we will hold fast to his promises.

If you seek to walk with God, you, too, will face tests of faith. Even Jesus faced tests, from the beginning of his ministry, when he entered the wilderness after his baptism, all the way to the end in the Garden of Gethsemane. You will most likely face multiple tests of your faith over the course of your life. James wrote these well-known words: "Consider it pure joy, my brothers, whenever you face trials of many kinds, because you know that the testing of your faith develops perseverance. Perseverance must finish its work so that you may be mature and complete, not lacking anything" (Jas. 1:2–4). Perseverance is one of the qualities that Peter admonishes us to increase. We'll delve deeper into what that means in a later chapter.

The test of faith ultimately boils down to this: Do we believe the truth about God? When we experience loss or tragedy or unfairness, does it change what we believe about God? In times of suffering, do we still believe that he is good? When we feel alone and deserted, do we believe that his promise never to leave us still holds true? Do we believe the time will come when Christ returns and establishes his kingdom on earth as well as in heaven?

The book of Job is an extended poetic parable that centers on questions like these. Job was a good and righteous man, yet all that he had—family, possessions, reputation, and even his health—was brutally stripped away. Job knew that his righteousness didn't deserve such a return. So, what did he believe about God after this? Job's honest wrestling with that question is the focus of the book about him.

Ancient philosophers wrote of courage as one of the cardinal virtues. The word *cardinal* comes from the Latin word *cardo*, which means "hinge." Therefore, a cardinal virtue is one that other virtues hinge upon. Faith is the cardinal virtue for the Christ-follower. It is not for the faint of heart.

Faith provides our rationale for the courage, perseverance, and discipline that enable us to practice the goodness to which Christ calls us. Because God exists, and because he is good, loving and faithful, we can have the moral courage to persevere in the face of difficulties and even disasters. Such courage doesn't spring fully formed from the mind and heart of a new Christ-follower. Rather, it is developed over time as Christians respond in faith to their trials.

Jesus himself was sustained by God's promises so that he could submit to his father's will and go through with his agonizing death on the cross: "Jesus, the author and perfecter of our faith, who for the joy set before him endured the cross" (Heb. 12:2). Jesus knew what God had promised him, and he held onto that promise even while suffering. And, just as Jesus "endured the cross," we all have our own trials to endure.

The writer of Hebrews exhorts us with these words: "So do not throw away your confidence; it will be richly rewarded. You need to persevere so that when you have done the will of God, you will receive what he has promised. For in just a very little while, 'He who is coming will come and will not delay. But my righteous one will live by faith. And if he shrinks back, I will not be pleased with him'" Heb. 10:35-38.

We are all tempted to "shrink back" when facing opposition, difficulties, and pain. We are encouraged instead to "live by faith." In other words, *faith is more than belief alone—it is belief expressed in action*. It empowers us to move forward when we feel like shrinking back.

Faith is sometimes depicted as an irrational response that closes its eyes to reality. Faith is not irrational, and it doesn't ignore the facts. Faith does not deny harsh realities; instead, it seeks to know and to ground itself on the foundation of reality by reminding us of those factors that we cannot see, weigh, or understand. Faith enables us to bring the truth about God into account as we weigh the factors in a difficult circumstance or a difficult decision.

A few years back, I read Rick Atkinson's *The Day of Battle*, a history of the Italian campaign mounted by American and British forces during the Second World War.[5] It was a brutal and costly campaign. The German army had fortified their positions in the mountains that form the spine of the Italian peninsula. The American and British troops had to fight their way from the beaches where they landed, all the way up those mountain heights. They had to drive the German forces from their well-defended positions one at a time. The human cost of this endeavor was horrific.

As the Allies finally neared Rome, the goal of a long campaign, German resistance was stiffening. The advancing American VI Corps came upon a fortified ridge at Velletri. If they could breach the German position there, they would be on the Germans' flank and could force a general retreat. While the American commander, General Lucian Truscott, pondered ways to push the Germans out, American scouts found an unguarded path up a steep slope behind the German position. If American troops could reach the top of the ridge before being discovered, the German force would be surrounded and subjected to fire on all sides.

But the German forces were too powerful for a small group of riflemen to defeat. Tanks and artillery would be needed on top of the ridge, and it would take time to get them in position. For such a surprise to succeed, the Germans' attention would need to be diverted.

Truscott decided to send a major portion of his forces straight up the hill in a frontal attack. The goal was to make the German garrison think they were facing the real attack in front of their position. Meanwhile, another column of troops would creep up the back of the ridge, undetected.

His tactic worked.

The forces Truscott sent up the back of the ridge both surprised and overwhelmed the outposts in the rear of the German position. The German forces were surrounded. In the struggle to escape, the German 362nd Infantry Division lost over half its fighting strength. When the battle was over, Truscott's army had punched a five-mile-deep hole in the German line, opening the door to Rome.

This overview of the battle for Velletri makes for a nice story. It seems clear that General Truscott made the right decision that day, as it resulted in victory. Imagine for a moment, though, that you had been one of those soldiers ordered to make the frontal attack on Velletri, exposed to the full weight of firepower from a crack German division. It wouldn't have taken long to realize you had no chance to take that hill.

That attack must have seemed senseless to the American soldiers who tried to advance up that hill, every wound and life lost a tragic waste. If you had been in their place, would you have thought your commanders had blundered?

Of course, the soldiers engaged in the frontal assault didn't have all the information needed to understand the mission assigned to them. But this raises a more difficult question: even if you knew of the greater plan, would you willingly lay down your life so that other soldiers could have an easier path to victory? In retrospect, we can see that the seemingly futile frontal assault on Velletri played an essential role in winning the battle. The troops who made the assault, however, paid a daunting price.

When I read Atkinson's book, I was going through the hardest time of my life. I was the CEO and primary owner for an architectural glass manufacturer based in Charleston, South Carolina. In the spring of 2007, after more than a decade of steady growth, we opened a new plant in Jacksonville, Florida. One month after the Jacksonville plant opened, the economy began its steep decline into the Great Recession of 2008–09. Within months, I found myself fighting to keep the company alive.

Florida was the epicenter of the real estate downturn in those years. Not only did new construction come to a sudden halt, but the financial impact of unsold homes rippled through the supply chain. Many long-time customers could no longer pay their bills. For two and a half years, I did everything I could to keep the company afloat—cut costs, shifted resources across markets, and leveraged our balance sheet with lenders and suppliers as far as it could stretch.

During this period, my home was also under duress. My wife was emerging from a near fatal bout with a rare blood disease. To protect her, I put enough cash to cover a year's expenses in an account in her name. I took the rest of our savings and put them back into the business, believing that the people who had invested with me deserved my one hundred percent commitment. I also didn't want to wonder for the rest of my life whether the company would have survived if I'd only had the courage to go "all in" during the crisis.

Losses accelerated after I made this final investment, and the funds were washed away in a few months. The final blow came early one morning. I was awakened at four o'clock by a call from our plant manager in Jacksonville. There had been an explosion. I learned that the plant's tempering oven—the key piece of equipment that processed virtually all the plant's finished products—had been disabled. Within the hour, I was on the road to Jacksonville.

When glass is tempered, it first passes through an oven chamber that heats the glass until it is soft. The red-hot glass then passes into a section of the oven called the quench, where it is blasted with cold air at high pressures. This causes the rapidly cooling surface of the glass to compress around the still-hot core, binding in tremendous energy. The compression is what makes tempered glass so hard. To create the air pressure needed for the process to work, the quench contains a component that looks like an old-time mill wheel, except it is made from thick steel plate. The wheel rotates at high speeds when the quench is in operation, driving the air pressure needed to cool the surface of the glass almost instantly.

That night, while the oven was operating, the wheel had suddenly disintegrated. Shards of thick steel plate tore through the oven and embedded themselves in the thick concrete walls that enclosed the quench. The enclosure had been built for sound protection, but it may have saved lives that night.

Ironically, just one week before the explosion occurred, the oven had been inspected by a technician from the factory where it was built. We had contracted to receive regular factory maintenance check-ups at the time we purchased the new oven. Though the technician was on site for two days, he never opened the enclosure to examine the quench wheel inside. Why would he, though? The wheel was a part that shouldn't fail in a hundred years.

After spending a few hours meeting with the team in Jacksonville, I drove back to Charleston. I spent the entire four-hour trip talking on the phone with bankers, attorneys, and our management team. As I gradually absorbed the implications of what had happened that night, it magnified a feeling that had been growing for months. I felt as if I'd been abandoned to spiritual attack, and in a way that I had never experienced before.

Do you remember the passage in Job where God asks Satan, "'Have you considered my servant Job?. . . he is blameless and upright.'" Then Satan responds, "'Does Job fear God for nothing? Have you not put a hedge around him and his household and everything he has? . . . stretch out your hand and strike everything he has, and he will surely curse you to your face'" (Job 1:8–11).

God agrees to remove his hedge of protection, making Job vulnerable to Satan's attacks. It's then that Job's suffering begins. This is how I felt during the crisis with my company—as if I was under assault from every side, both professionally and personally. Many companies struggled with the impact of recession, but with all that I experienced, it felt like I was being buffeted by more than just hard economic times. The bizarre tempering oven explosion was only one of a series of unusual events that magnified the impact of the deep economic downturn on our business.

My feelings were intensified by the importance of this role in my life. After fourteen years, I had come to view leading my company as my life's work.

I read about that battle at Velletri a few days after the oven explosion at the plant. As I imagined how those soldiers must have felt, taking part in that doomed frontal assault, I sensed God asking me: What about you? What if that's your role in my ultimate victory, to be shot down on a hill you have no chance of taking? Are you willing to do that for me? The directness of the question stunned me like a punch in the jaw.

As I thought about it in the days that followed, I realized that this question framed God's challenge for me. Was I willing to accept the destruction of my life's work, if that was asked, just as Christ had laid down his life for me? Could I do it gratefully and not grudgingly? Would I still believe that God was good? Could I believe that my loss was not a waste, and there was a joy ahead of me that would be worth it all?

It has often seemed to me that our churches' teaching mostly centers on victories—on faith stories that offer happy endings. In my experience, the happy endings must often be taken in faith, because the outcome we see isn't a happy one.

My story with the glass company didn't have a happy ending. After the explosion of the Jacksonville tempering oven, the company was no longer viable. The bank called in our loans within a month, forcing me to liquidate the company. This is the most painful loss that I have ever experienced. All that I had worked to build for fifteen years was ripped away, and I struggled to understand why God allowed it to happen.

At the time I was forced to close my business, I had led it for nearly as many years as my daughter, my youngest child, had been alive. When the company ceased to exist, it felt as though a child of mine had died. In such a situation, it is hard to forgive yourself, because you can always point to mistakes made along the way. You always wonder, *what if I had . . .?* Time tempers grief and loss, but the questions are still there.

I closed the business fifteen years ago. In the aftermath, I had to reinvent myself professionally and start over financially. I suppose that I have succeeded. I found meaningful work that draws on skills I'd developed over the years and have found many opportunities to be useful. However, though the pain of those years of loss has faded, it hasn't disappeared. I sometimes struggle with the sense that the work I do now is less significant than the work I lost, and I wonder, *has God relegated me to a backwater because I failed his test in some way?* Although I move on, this thought doesn't feel like victory to me. I may not have lost a child, but at times I feel like the partially disabled survivor of an accident or disease.

I realize that I may not see the true significance of my work. The culture-influenced values that we use to gauge significance differ in crucial ways from the biblical standard. God knows all, while we do not. I strive to live in the faith that his ways are better than mine and to be at peace with my circumstances and my future.

Friends who know my story have sometimes praised my level of faith during and after my crisis. What stands out to me, though, when I look back on those hard times is not my faith but God's faithfulness.

A. W. Tozer was an American Christian pastor, author, magazine editor, and spiritual mentor. He wrote these words: "Faith creates nothing; it simply reckons upon that which is already there."[6] And he was right. Moreover, we learn to reckon on what is there through experience, not through education. I experienced the worst that I could have imagined, and I see in retrospect that God was with me the whole time. He provided for my needs throughout the process of liquidating the business, then opened the door for consulting work immediately after. My wife and I always had enough, even though her health care costs were very high at that time. I was able to resolve portions of the company's indebtedness that could have created crushing longer-term burdens in a way that, in retrospect, seems miraculous. God blessed work relationships. I remember coming out of a meeting with bankers to whom the company owed millions of dollars. The meeting was amicable and productive, and an attorney I knew only slightly was shaking his head as we came out of the meeting. "That's the way meetings like that should go, and never do," he said.

As I went through the process, I saw God's hand at work in many circumstances—small things, for the most part, that seemed incidental to the one big thing that was consuming my attention. I believe God wanted to show me that, though my prayers for the business's survival were unanswered, he was never absent or inattentive to me. By providing repeated instances of his love and care, reminding me that he was fully aware of each step in the process, I could see that God was allowing me to lose my business for a purpose, though I didn't (and still don't) know what that purpose was.

One reason I struggle to find spiritual meaning in my loss is that I don't see how my suffering served God. After all, it's not as if I was being persecuted for my faith. And we all know that businesses fail all the time.

But when I look beyond the surface of events, I glimpse a different picture. I know that the Bible teaches that our faith is precious to God. In some way, when we continue to believe the truth about God even when our circumstances test that belief, it honors and pleases him. Earlier I quoted this passage from the book of James: "The testing of your faith develops perseverance. Perseverance must finish its work so that you may be mature and complete, not lacking anything" (Jas. 1:3–4). In the years since closing the business, I have been able to persevere in centering my relationships and my work on a foundation of faith. I can say that I have persevered, though I'm sure that perseverance has not yet finished its work in my life.

I still feel pain from that loss, as I still feel twinges from a bad injury to my right leg that happened years ago. To live with permanent damage from an injury or loss doesn't rob life of all its sweetness. It may limit one's range of activity, but there are many other channels into which we can pour our energy. I can be at peace with my loss—the same peace I saw in my father—no matter what I see ahead, because I know from experience that God will be with me. As the best known of Psalms expresses it, "Even though I walk through the valley of the shadow of death, I will fear no evil, for you are with me" (Ps. 23:4).

Holding fast to the truth when we are suffering—learning to reckon on our God who is there—builds a resilience into our faith that could never develop during good times alone. This kind of faith reaches beyond the beliefs we hold in our minds and emotions.

As James wrote, we show our faith by what we do (Jas. 2:18). To embody love, knowledge, and goodness demands both hard work and sacrifice, but that investment enables our lives to bear fruit.

Faith sometimes requires that we serve others who cannot, or will not, reciprocate. It compels us to work for peace, to treat others' concerns as equal to our own, and to put aside our right to fight for what we believe is ours. Faith enables us to charge a fortified hill, a hill we have no chance of taking, if that is the role assigned. What God asks of us is the most important thing for us to do. What he chooses to strip away is less important, no matter how it feels, because God is the one who sees and knows what is truly important.

A person must have strong reasons to live sacrificially. To justify transcendent claims on our lives requires reasons that transcend any motivation that can come from within. Our faith in God's great and precious promises provides those reasons. Faith is rooted in a transcendent God. Faith trusts in God's promise to love and care for us without end. In turn, God, in his goodness, "has given us everything we need for life and godliness through our knowledge of him" (2 Pet. 1:3). Faith, then, is the *foundation* for character.

Let's talk next about how we build upon that foundation.

chapter four

Goodness

*For this very reason, make every effort
to add to your faith **goodness** . . .*
2 PETER 1:5

t the outset of this book, I quoted a line from Søren Kierkegaard's
journal, written shortly after his conversion experience: "Now,
with God's help, I shall become myself."[7] Kierkegaard's words
capture the essence of what Peter means when he tells us, "Make every
effort to add to your faith *goodness*." If that connection seems surprising,
stick with me while I explain.

If you have studied the literature or philosophy of the ancient
Greeks, you may recognize the Greek word Peter uses that is translated
as "goodness"—*areté*. In classical studies, it is most often translated as
"virtue." The word *virtue* suggests aspects of Peter's meaning that the
word *goodness* does not fully capture.

But *virtue* is also a Rorschach word (I assume you're familiar with
the inkblot test, which has been a standard clinical diagnostic tool in

psychiatry for over 100 years, testing a person's personality by their interpretation of inkblots). In other words, what the word *virtue* means to us depends more on what we project onto it than on the dictionary definition. In our culture, virtue can have priggish connotations that convey something other than what Peter means.

Paul uses *areté* in Philippians 4:8 in a context that gives a more rounded sense of the word's meaning: "Finally, brothers, whatever is true, whatever is noble, whatever is right, whatever is pure, whatever is lovely, whatever is admirable—if anything is excellent [*areté*] or praiseworthy—think about such things."

Areté describes what is intrinsically good in a person or thing, what makes them preeminent among their peers. You could say, as Kierkegaard's journal entry suggests, that *areté* describes the extent to which someone or something fulfills its potential. When Peter tells us to "make every effort to add to your faith, *areté*," he is saying that *each of us is to fulfill the potential for excellence that God has given us.*

The shape that goodness takes and the way we express goodness in action will be different for each of us, because each of us reflects God's image in a unique way. When we build goodness on a foundation of faith, we grow into the potential that God has given us. Jesus said it this way: "I will show you what he is like who comes to me and hears my words and puts them into practice. He is like a man building a house, who dug down deep and laid the foundation on rock. When a flood came, the torrent struck that house but could not shake it" (Luke 6:47–48).

Evangelical teaching often undervalues goodness, either by focusing on faith alone or by translating goodness into purely theological terms that rob the word of its living meaning. We have an understandable desire to avoid a religion based on good works. Protestant theology teaches that we are saved by faith alone, apart from works. This is biblical and true: "For it is by grace you have been saved, through faith—and this not from yourselves, it is the gift of God—not by works, so that no one can boast" (Eph. 2:8–9).

Other faith traditions view salvation more as a lifelong process of drawing near to God, often referred to as sanctification. This is also biblical and true. Unless our lives express the power of God's Spirit working through us, and unless it changes how we live and think and act, faith is dead. "What good is it, my brothers, if a man claims to have faith but has no deeds? Can such faith save him?" (Jas. 2:14).

These two principles do not contradict each other. Instead, they express different aspects of goodness that should be true for each of us. We are to make every effort to blend a hope-producing faith with the fruit of a life well-lived. Faith should make us faithful. Love and faith will inevitably be expressed by acts of kindness, helpfulness, and service. Unless these things are visible in a person's life, it must be questioned whether love and faith reside there. Conversely, if love and faith reside in you, they will be visible.

If our love is not visible, we are wise to question whether our faith is real. John puts it bluntly in this passage:

> This is how we know what love is: Jesus Christ laid down his life for us. And we ought to lay down our lives for our brothers. If anyone has material possessions and sees his brother in need but has no pity on him, how can the love of God be in him? Dear children, let us not love with words or tongue but with actions and in truth. (1 John 3:16–18)

Before we go further, we need to consider another aspect of biblical teaching on goodness. As we have seen, *areté* conveys an aspirational aspect of goodness; God has endowed each of us with potential and we are to develop what he has given us. This aspect of goodness focuses on excellence. Other biblical teaching centers on moral goodness. When Jesus teaches that "every good tree bears good fruit, but a bad tree bears bad fruit. A good tree cannot bear bad fruit, and a bad tree cannot bear good fruit" (Matt. 7:17–18), he uses the Greek words *agathos* and *kalos*. Used together, these words convey "goodness" as a function of intrinsic moral rootedness that is naturally expressed through action that is beneficial to others.

These words for "goodness" are used more often in the New Testament than *areté*. They add another dimension to the meaning of the word. Goodness denotes excellence, the fulfilling of a person's potential, but it also denotes the consistency that produces good moral fruit season after season.

Our discussion begs the question: Why aren't more of us good? The very nature of religion provides one reason. The prevailing idea in primitive religions was to appease gods who could be deceived by external compliance or who could be influenced by gifts to grant favor. Even today, many religions emphasize external compliance with a set of rules and ritual behaviors. Judaism marked a break with that approach. The God of the Bible is pleased when our lives express justice and mercy. Micah 6:8 captures this teaching memorably: "He has showed you, O man, what is good. And what does the Lord require of you? To act justly and to love mercy and to walk humbly with your God."

This definition of good is easy to understand, even as it is profoundly difficult to follow. As a result, we all remain vulnerable to the religious impulse to find safety in setting and complying with rules; for this reason, religion has pervaded human experience throughout history.

In Jesus' day, the practice of Judaism had increasingly centered on external compliance with God's commands rather than on the attitude of the heart. The Pharisees centered their serious study of religion on stringent literal interpretations of the Law of Moses. As Jesus observed, the Pharisees took the command to tithe so seriously that they even culled and contributed ten percent of the herbs that grew in their kitchen gardens (Matt. 23:23). The Pharisees extended this kind of rulemaking in so many areas that the average Jew couldn't possibly keep up with all their rules, and the Pharisees' knowledge of and compliance with these rules became a point of pride—it set them apart as the "godliest" members of their communities. When an aspect of religion becomes a point of pride, you can be certain it has taken you off track. Jesus pointed his followers in the opposite direction, teaching them to cultivate worshipful, just, merciful, and humble hearts.

If we would avoid barren lives, we must understand the implications of Jesus' critique of the Pharisees. After all, the Pharisees were arguably the most dedicated Jews of their time. Their sect contained serious scholars who knew the Scriptures as well as anyone. Gamaliel, the Pharisee under whom the Apostle Paul studied, is still considered one of the greatest Jewish teachers.

To counter the tendency of religion to metastasize into a thicket of rules, Jesus tells us to love God with our whole hearts. I've heard it said many times that the Bible provides a roadmap for life, but I think this metaphor is misleading. Instead of providing a map, the Bible tells us how to stay close to the Guide. After all, if you have a map, then you don't need a guide. But we are to walk with Christ. Staying close to the Guide is the only important thing. It is everything. The aspirational goodness promoted by Scripture is the kind that seeks to grow in relationship to the Guide and become like him. It seeks to grow into maturity in Christ, as we've discussed.

To explore how walking with Christ forms goodness in us, let's look again at Philippians 4:8: "Whatever is true, whatever is noble, whatever is right, whatever is pure, whatever is lovely, whatever is admirable—if anything is excellent or praiseworthy—think about such things."

Meditating on these things enables us to further our understanding of what best produces lives that are superabundant with goodness. Yet for too many of us, our knowledge of the good fails to guide our actions.

The years I've spent working in manufacturing plants have shown me that we often confuse education with training. Imagine that I see a group of production workers handling material in a way that could lead to damage. If I tell them why the method is wrong and then walk away, I have educated them. But I have learned that when I stop there, the behavior is unlikely to change. Production workers need more from me than information; they need to be trained in the right method.

Consider how the United States Marines turn recruits into soldiers who can perform effectively in combat. They don't merely educate recruits, they train them. When a soldier is in danger and adrenaline surges through their body, it isn't possible to think calmly or carefully about the best way to respond. Soldiers need to make the right response automatically. Repetitive training equips them to do that.

Though few of us will face the kind of danger a soldier faces in combat, the challenges are analogous. We need to respond correctly when powerful emotions surge through our bodies, or when external pressures tug us in the wrong direction. Sometimes those pressures even come from those we love. We need to train ourselves in the habits of choosing and acting rightly and wisely.

And we need to remember that we will always be incapable of responding rightly if we rely solely on our own strength. Jesus underscores this truth, telling us: "I am the vine; you are the branches. If a man remains in me and I in him, he will bear much fruit; apart from me you can do nothing" (John 15:5). Do you see why we need to stay close to the Guide?

When we experience another person's goodness, it is because that person's behavior proceeds authentically from a life lived in communion with God.

Goodness must be authentic. Being authentic means that your character is open for others to see, that you haven't hidden or disguised who you are. In other words, the persona you present to others is not at odds with the qualities of character you embody. Without authenticity, any goodness a person seems to possess is apparent but not real.

Integrity is another word often used in this context. Sometimes, we equate integrity with honesty, but integrity encompasses far more than honesty. The word *integrity* shares the same root as the word *integrated*. It means you are the same through and through, that who you are on the inside and who you are on the outside are entirely consistent. Accordingly, we violate integrity any time our actions express the false self we wish to project, rather than the self that truly is.

In the same way that integrity encompasses honesty but means something more, authenticity encompasses integrity, yet it, too, means something more. Philosopher Simon Blackburn describes authenticity in this way: "[It] is not merely a correspondence between inner thought and outer expression, although it implies at least that much. *It requires in addition an achievement within the self. It requires deep self-knowledge or deep self-awareness, coupled with a determination to express that self in choices, actions, inclinations, or feelings*"[8] (emphasis added).

By coupling self-awareness with integrity, authenticity allows an inner freedom. Authentic people have taken control of their identity. They resist the scripts their culture and community write for them and can instead craft identities that are founded on self-discovery. A person who lacks self-awareness may exhibit integrity but will have a limited ability to sustain healthy relationships. Unless actions express an inner reality, they cannot be received or felt as truly intended.

Self-discovery encompasses a further dimension when we evaluate it through the lens of faith. As Christians, we seek to discover not just who we are and how we are wired, but who we are in relationship to God.

This is not a small matter, nor is it easy to accomplish. We are told, "The heart is deceitful above all things and beyond cure. Who can understand it?" (Jer. 17:9). There is much to overcome within ourselves before we can see ourselves as we are. We judge other people by what they do, but we judge ourselves by what we intend—a much more lenient standard. Most people aspire to have a positive and loving impact on the lives they touch, but there is always a gap between the love we seek to express and how people experience us.

The Puritan theologian John Owen wrote that most people remain strangers to themselves; "they give flattering names to their own natural weaknesses. They try to justify, palliate, or excuse the evils of their own hearts, . . . They never gain a realistic view of themselves."[9] Do not comfort yourself that your intentions are positive and that is enough. Everyone who is not a sociopath has good intentions. The test is whether you consistently act in ways that fulfill those good intentions.

We are weak, needy, deeply flawed beings—but we also have vast potential for excellence and moral goodness, which can be developed through a relationship with the God who created us and who loves our souls. God's response to Jeremiah's lament over the deceitful human heart is answered, "I the Lord search the heart and examine the mind, to reward a man according to his conduct, according to what his deeds deserve" (Jer. 17:10).

I love the way J. B. Phillips translates Romans 12:2: "Don't let the world around you squeeze you into its own mould but let God re-mould your minds from within."[10] When we can see ourselves and the world around us clearly, without the perceptual distortions produced by cultural and societal pressures, "then [we] will be able to test and approve what God's will is—his good, pleasing and perfect will" (Rom. 12:2).

Jesus lived authentically in this sense. He was an utterly original human being, always surprising the people around him, even those closest to him, because he spoke and acted in response to God's Spirit and wasn't bound by the expectations or assumptions of the culture or the religious environment in which he lived. It's interesting, too, to notice that what he condemned more often than anything else in the Pharisees and other religious leaders of his day was their hypocrisy. He called them "whitewashed tombs" (Matt. 23:27), presenting an image of goodness that covered over a foul reality.

A great deal of biblical teaching focuses on developing godly character. Ironically, we often seek to put these teachings into practice by putting on a mask. We try to disguise ourselves rather than choosing to change ourselves.

Jesus says, "Do not worry" (Matt. 6:25). And so we do our best not to seem worried. But Jesus isn't talking about the masks we wear. He's referring to the real person behind the mask. He's not interested in whether we can *project* calmness, as I sought to do as a young man trying to emulate my father. Rather, Jesus wants us to experience real peace.

Of course, we all wear masks sometimes; we wear some masks every day. We may want other people to think that we are powerful or smart or good; that we are successful and affluent; that our marriages are solid; that our children are talented and well-adjusted; or that we have many friends. Too often, we *pretend* that we are good; we hide our flaws rather than acknowledge them.

The temptation to wear a mask can take subtle forms. I am too self-conscious, too aware of Jesus' teaching, to readily wear a mask of pretense while posting photos of my perfect life on a Facebook page. Instead, I wear the mask of privacy. This is a mask that feels natural to me, because I am by nature a private person. However, this approach also creates barriers to real and honest relationships.

I began my working career with a global company. By my early thirties, I had worked my way up to the fringe of executive leadership.

One night, during a strategic planning retreat for the executive team, I sat beside a senior leader at dinner. We talked for most of the evening.

The next day, my boss caught up with me during a break between meetings.

"Hey, I was watching you as you talked with Dave last night," he said.

And I was prepared for a compliment because I thought my conversation with this leader had gone quite well. But his next words took me by surprise.

"Let me tell you something I observed," he continued. "You kept Dave engaged all evening talking about his stuff, but you never talked about yourself. You always turned the conversation back to him. It was skillfully done, and I don't know that he even noticed, but if you never share anything about yourself, if no one ever gets to know Jack, then no one will be able to trust you."

My boss was telling me that healthy relationships require mutuality. Even when the masks we wear aren't meant to deceive, they still prevent the open give-and-take needed to build healthy relationships that can endure stresses and strains, and that enable us to sharpen one another (Prov. 27:17). Goodness is deeply personal, because it is expressed in ways that flow from each person's unique individuality.

We cannot mask our true selves in the long run. Lack of authenticity is inevitably revealed. People are quick to detect insincerity, because it is so often used to manipulate, and our need for self-preservation drives most of us to be perpetually alert for signs that someone is trying to nudge us in one direction or another. Furthermore, the masks we wear tend to slip as soon as we are under pressure. As Jesus shrewdly noted, "Out of the overflow of the heart the mouth speaks" (Matt. 12:34). Healthy, lasting relationships cannot be founded on a lie. If your actions do not proceed from love, they cannot be sustained.

I wrote earlier that doing good is inseparable from *being* good. Ultimately, we can't *do* good consistently unless we *are* good. But the line of thought we have just been following means that the converse is also true: unless you are *doing* good, you are deluding yourself to think that you *are* good. The New Testament letter from James hammers this point home with brutal directness:

- Do not merely listen to the word, and so deceive yourselves. Do what it says. (Jas. 1:22)
- Faith without deeds is useless. (Jas. 2:20)
- Who is wise and understanding among you? Let him show it by his good life, by deeds done in the humility that comes from wisdom. (Jas. 3:13)

James's words are not written to discourage us—quite the contrary. We *can* do what the Word says: our faith *can* be expressed in deeds; the humility that comes from wisdom *can* produce a good life. As Paul explains, these words are written to teach us, so that "through endurance and the encouragement of the Scriptures we might have hope" (Rom. 15:4).

How do we live authentically and express God's Word through our actions? Let's talk about this concept next.

chapter five

Knowledge

*. . . and to goodness, **knowledge** . . .*
2 PETER 1:5

Typically, when we think about knowledge in spiritual terms, our first thoughts are that we wish to know God's will for our lives. Discerning God's will for us is an essential outcome of knowledge, and it is critical that we seek it. However, we often look in the wrong place for this knowledge; we look into the future rather than at the present.

Our spiritual life powerfully shapes our view of the future. Faith grows out of experience—the past—and guides how we interpret events and circumstances as we live through them in the present. Faith also frames our beliefs about what lies ahead. But while faith can enable us to enter the future with confidence, we don't know what the future will bring. Paul wrote that our knowledge is "but a poor reflection as in a mirror" (1 Cor. 13:12).

In the church, we often talk about "waiting on the Lord," sometimes implying that God will give specific guidance for every step we are to take. Many evangelical Christians maintain the belief that this is the only spiritual way for people to live—that this "wait" is required if we are to live in accordance with God's will rather than our own will, relying upon his power rather than on our own means.

However, this belief can lead us to act as though God is a genie in a lamp, compelled to answer our questions if we rub the lamp in the prescribed way. When we read Scripture passages that describe how God responds to prayer, we sometimes interpret the words of those passages as if they are incantations that, if repeated correctly, ensure that God will tell us what we want to know.

The thing we misunderstand is that God's will for us does not necessarily hinge on where we work, or where we live, or which product we buy, or any other practical matters that require decisions from us. Rather, *God's will is that we walk with him every moment of every day.* In Ephesians 5, Paul admonishes us, "Be very careful, then, how you live—not as unwise, but as wise, making the most of every opportunity, because the days are evil. Therefore do not be foolish, but *understand what the Lord's will is*" (Eph. 5:15–17, emphasis added).

And what is the Lord's will? "Live a life of love, just as Christ loved us and gave himself up for us . . . be filled with the Spirit" (Eph. 5:2, 18).

When I reflect on times when I have sensed God guiding me, that guidance has almost always related to the moment I found myself in rather than providing information about the future. And when I walk through my days with God, actively seeking to be aware of his presence, I often discern him prompting me to reach out to others through kindness, love, and concern. God's will for us is expressed as we live obediently in the present; the future will come in its time. As Jesus put it, "Do not worry about tomorrow, for tomorrow will worry about itself" (Matt. 6:34).

God does care about the decisions that concern us. However, his method of guiding our decisions rarely involves telling us what to do. Instead, God wants us to become wise.

- Psalm 111 tells us that "The fear of the Lord is the beginning of wisdom."
- Proverbs 4:7 counsels us, "Wisdom is supreme; therefore get wisdom. Though it cost all you have, get understanding."
- Proverbs 3:13 and 15 say, "Blessed is the man who finds wisdom, the man who gains understanding . . . She is more precious than rubies; nothing you desire can compare with her."

All wisdom is rooted in the realization that God is over all and that he wants us to serve him with our hearts, minds, and souls.

James 1:5 is often quoted as a teaching on how God guides us: "If any of you lacks wisdom, he should ask God, who gives generously to all without finding fault." James doesn't say that God will give us answers; he says that God will give us wisdom. Yes, God wants to guide us, but he most often does so by enabling us to live wisely and choose wisely. In other words, we should be seeking knowledge that will lead us to faithful living and to loving relationships.

We are not capable of this on our own. We must first see God clearly and love him well.

A. W. Tozer begins his classic book *The Knowledge of the Holy* with these penetrating words: "What comes into our minds when we think about God is the most important thing about us."[11] He argues that it is impossible for a person or a culture to rise above their idea of God. "We tend by a secret law of the soul to move toward our mental image of God."[12] If a person believes in, worships, and serves a god who is petty, mean, and cruel, it is unimaginable that he or she will be large-hearted, kind, and generous.

The issue, of course, is not to create a god in our own image; it is to have a concept of God that corresponds as closely as possible to the God who is. If God created all that is and sustains it moment by moment, and "in him we live and move and have our being" (Acts 17:28), then the more accurate our concept of God is, the more clear-sighted we will be. Furthermore, if the God we serve is holy, worthy, and true—a God whose goodness and love were revealed through the life of Jesus Christ—then we can grow in holiness, worth, and truth as we follow Him.

God's will for us in every situation is that we express love through action. His will can only be discerned in his living presence, and our ability to walk in accordance with his will comes through his grace, which must be constantly renewed in us. In other words, we learn God's will in the present as we abide in him and he enables us to live lovingly in the present.

The knowledge that God wants us to seek is a knowledge that nourishes maturity. It is a commonly accepted that the noble ideals young people bring with them cannot survive adulthood. Don't believe this. People don't give up on their ideals because those ideals aren't realistic. They give up because their ideals are too hard, far harder to achieve than they'd ever imagined. In the same way, the walk of faith proves to be difficult in different ways than we expected at the beginning of our journey. I write this not to discourage you but to prepare you. And let me assure you: the walk of faith is far more rewarding than we can imagine when we begin; it is worth the rigors of the journey.

Hebrews 5:14 teaches that mature believers "by constant use have trained themselves to distinguish good from evil." The knowledge of good and evil, then, is not something we learn by memorizing rules once and for all. Instead, it requires the wise and constant application of love to each situation and each person.

Note, too, that the biblical focus is on knowledge that informs our behavior. Paul warned often against the acquisition of spiritual knowledge for its own sake. He pointed out that "knowledge puffs up, but love builds up. The man who thinks he knows something does not yet know as he ought to know" (1 Cor. 8:1–2). In his letter to the young pastor Timothy, Paul warns against those who have "an unhealthy interest in controversies and quarrels about words that result in envy, strife, malicious talk, evil suspicions and constant friction" (1 Tim. 6:4–5).

There is nothing wrong with sound doctrine. But the knowledge that Peter exhorts us to grasp has a different orientation. This knowledge produces humility, not arrogance. It enables us to live wisely and powerfully in the moment. We can face loss, grief, failure, or a fearsome future and live valiantly and love selflessly in the face of it. We can do this because we are armed with the knowledge that God's purpose for us cannot be thwarted, and that nothing can separate us from his enduring, unshakable love. This knowledge guides us along the path that is marked out for us. We may not know what comes next, but we can know all that is needed to live with love and contentment in the present.

Sometimes, though, this process of walking with God looks different from what we imagined. We often assume that growing in spiritual maturity means growing ever closer to God. That's true, but I think we can misunderstand what closeness to God looks like.

Here's a personal example. In some ways, I am now closer to my mother than I have ever been. In the first years after my dad passed away, she and I were together more than any time since I had left for college. Each year since then has brought more shared experiences and new passages in life for both of us. However, it would be difficult to say that our relationship is closer than it was when I was an infant and lived in her arms. The closeness that we share as adults is completely different from when I was a baby, completely dependent on her.

I would guess few would say that growing up is a bad thing. All parents want their children to grow and mature into responsible, well-adjusted adults who can live independently. Children, in turn, continually stretch for independence as they grow.

I have so enjoyed seeing my children step into the challenges and opportunities that life presents, as they learn to understand themselves and their potential and discern their path in life. Those are all good steps. However, the process is bittersweet for a parent; those steps of maturity have taken my children farther away from me in some respects. They live in their own homes now, not mine; two of them live in different cities where they are building their careers and their own families. But the relationships we have as mature adults are deeper and richer than they ever could have been when they were children. Maturity is a beautiful thing, and it is what we were meant to pursue and achieve.

Likewise, maturity is what God wants for every one of us.

For a person to mature, their parents, both earthly and spiritual, must allow enough distance so that they learn to exercise independence. A baby may panic if she can't see her parents. This is a normal reaction, without cause for concern. But any parent would be rightfully alarmed if her sixteen-year-old displayed the same reaction. We help our children become independent by encouraging them to leave our orbit and develop an orbit of their own—gradually, over time, and in appropriate ways adapted to their stage of maturity and independence.

In the same way, as we mature, we can expect times when God will guide us less rather than more. This picture of spiritual maturity may be at odds with the way you have visualized a growing relationship with the Lord. As we walk with him through the years, we anticipate growing closer to him. And we do. However, seasons of spiritual intimacy are inevitably interspersed with times when God seems distant, including occasions when we reach out in pain or confusion and sense no answer from him at all.

In his classic book *Spiritual Leadership*, J. Oswald Sanders, a prominent global missions leader for many years, shared a conversation he had with D. E. Hoste, who led the China Inland Mission in the first half of the twentieth century. This is what Hoste said to him, a testimony that connects the shared spiritual experience of three generations of godly missions leaders—Hoste, Hudson Taylor (the founder of the China Inland Mission and one of the most influential missions leaders in modern history), and Sanders himself:

> I more and more see that as we go on in the Christian life, the Lord very often does not want to give us the sense of his presence, or the consciousness of his help. There again Mr. Hudson Taylor helped me very much. We were talking about guidance. He said how in his younger days, things used to come so clearly, so quickly to him. "But," he said, "now as I have gone on, and God has used me more and more, I seem often to be like a man going along in a fog. I do not know what to do."[13]

If you seek after God with all your heart and pursue him steadily through the years, this may ultimately happen to you. When it does, do not lose faith in God's purpose for your life, which is to steadily shape us into the image of Christ. The separation from the Father that Jesus experienced on Calvary was devastatingly painful. Hanging on the cross, he cried out, "My God, my God, why have you forsaken me?" (Matt. 27:46). But Jesus was sustained in his obedience all through his humiliating death by "the joy set before him" (Heb. 12:2).

In the same way, when we experience suffering, hardship, or loss and we continue to trust in the goodness of God, our faith is treasured by a God who loves us immeasurably.

- "God is not unjust; he will not forget your work and the love you have shown him" (Heb. 6:10).
- "Therefore we do not lose heart . . . For our light and momentary troubles are achieving for us an eternal glory that far outweighs them all" (2 Cor. 4:16–17).

Knowledge, then, is not an end in itself; its purpose is instrumental, nourishing other qualities that enable us to become more like Christ. Knowledge helps sustain faith, and it nourishes maturity.

Equally important, knowledge lays the foundation for love. Read what Paul wrote to the Philippian church: "This is my prayer: *that your love may abound more and more in knowledge* and depth of insight, so that you may be able to discern what is best and may be pure and blameless until the day of Christ" (Phil. 1:9–10, emphasis added).

Does it seem strange that Paul links love with knowledge—"that your *love* may abound more and more in *knowledge*"? Much can be said about what Paul means by linking love and knowledge; earlier in the chapter we explored the importance of rooting our relationship with God in an accurate knowledge of him. The link between love and knowledge also applies to our human relationships.

Most of the time, we think about love as something apart from knowledge—as a powerful emotion based on feelings rather than discernment. This is because we have been taught that love is the ultimate subjective response, distorting our view of another person rather than bringing clarity. Let's see if you agree with these two statements:

- *God knows each of us accurately and fully.* This is part of what we mean when we say God is omniscient. Not only does he know everything, but his knowledge is accurate—indeed, definitive. If we could see as God sees, we would be seeing truly and completely.
- *God sees everyone with eyes of love.* John's gospel and his letters center on this truth. In fact, Jesus' last instruction to his disciples before his death on the cross was simply this: "Love each other" (John 15:17). He taught that if their love for God was real, they would demonstrate that love through obedience: "If anyone loves me, he will obey my teaching" (John 14.23).

If both statements are true, *love and knowledge are inseparable.* Far from distorting our view of reality, love provides the only lens that enables us to see another person clearly, for when we love we have the motive and energy to seek to know other people as they truly are. We see them with understanding and acceptance, able to celebrate their goodness and their gifts, even as we see and acknowledge their failings and flaws. We can extend the grace that comes from understanding, a grace that is sympathetic to weakness.

This is precisely the way God sees each of us. It is the truest, most accurate way in which we can be seen.

God's vision does not look past our flaws or ignore them. On the contrary, he sees them more clearly than we do. And still, he loves each person truly and equally and fully. This is one aspect of the "knowledge and depth of insight" (Phil. 1:9) that Paul urges us to grow into.

Several years ago, I was invited to speak at a campus ministry gathering for a local college. They asked me to talk about finding God's will for your life. If there is a more *apropos* college student topic, I don't know what it would be. Most college students are at the beginning of their adult years; they are wondering what life has in store for them and how to find their way.

I have come to think that the answers to questions like these are less important to God than they are to us. I told those students, "I've learned that when we ask God, 'What is your will for my life?', he's likely to answer, 'Here's my will for this afternoon. You do that, and we'll go from there.'"

The knowledge of God's will, expressed in our actions as we live in the present, is essential if we are to live lovingly and faithfully. But knowledge does not automatically produce consistent action. We need to develop self-control to live in accordance with the knowledge we have. Let's talk about this next.

chapter six

Self-Control

*. . . and to knowledge, **self-control** . . .*
2 PETER 1:6

f you grew up in the United States, you have been surrounded by messages that individuals should have the greatest possible freedom to make their own decisions.

Biblical teaching places a high value on freedom, though it describes freedom differently than our culture does. The Bible teaches that you are free if your words and actions consistently express love—as we saw in the previous chapter, a love that is informed by knowledge and depth of insight. We have defined character as embodying the capacity to live well; such a life consists of fully and consistently demonstrating love.

Sometimes our range of action is constrained by external factors. In our fallen world, there are times when no option seems good, while even the best available course of action is characterized by trade-offs. In addition to these external constraints on our freedom, our choices are also constrained internally. The flaws etched in each of us limit our freedom to choose the best. Paul teaches that these constraints are the enduring legacy of sin. He writes, "I am unspiritual, sold as a slave to sin . . . For what I do is not the good I want to do; no, the evil I do not want to do—this I keep on doing" (Rom. 7:14, 19).

But there is good news for us: God's Spirit gives us the power to emerge from being enslaved to sin into a life marked by fruitfulness— indeed, by power. As Paul explains, "Through Christ Jesus the law of the Spirit of life set me free from the law of sin and death" (Rom. 8:2).

How do we become truly free?

It may seem paradoxical, but *freedom grows from self-control*. Self-control expands our freedom by giving us the means to choose the path of love and to do so more consistently. Self-control is exercised as we take hold of the Spirit's power through faith.

This suggests that perhaps we should be thinking about self-control in a specific way. The self-control Peter speaks of is not self-repression, nor is it self-denial, though self-denial is part of the life to which Jesus calls us. Instead, the self-control Peter describes is like the discipline of an athlete preparing for competition. This metaphor permeates Paul's letters. Paul writes:

> Do you not know that in a race all the runners run, but only one gets the prize? Run in such a way as to get the prize. Everyone who competes in the games goes into strict training. They do it to get a crown that will not last; but we do it to get a crown that will last forever. (1 Cor. 9:24–25)

The word *agonizomai*, rendered "strict training" here, is another form of the word Peter uses for "self-control." The New American Standard Bible more literally translates verse 25 to read: "Everyone who competes in the games exercises self-control in all things."

In other words, self-control is how we focus all our energies on pursuing "the prize."

When, through faith, we set our sights on what the Spirit desires for us, we can access the power to live in accordance with what we see. Self-control and discipline develop our ability to take hold of this power that God's Spirit makes available to us. It is an arduous process, but faith fuels the perseverance that we need to "share in his [Christ's] sufferings in order that we may also share in his glory" (Rom. 8:17).

When we think about exercising self-control to pursue God's will, it seems natural to focus on our sin. Truly, we all have besetting sins. Each of us is particularly vulnerable to certain temptations, many of which are presented to us daily. We, in turn, must strangle them daily if we are to live in a way that is pleasing to God.

Strangle is a strong word, but strong measures are required. Paul expresses our internal conflict this way: "If you live according to the sinful nature, you will die; but if by the Spirit you *put to death* the misdeeds of the body, you will live" (Rom. 8:13, emphasis added). Spiritual life hinges on our response to sin.

Mindful of what is at stake, the writer of Hebrews exhorts us with these words, "'Today, if you hear his voice, do not harden your hearts'" (Heb. 3:7–8). It is always "today," every moment of our lives. We must discipline ourselves to listen for the Spirit's voice and, by his guidance and through his power, seek to live consistently in each "today" as it comes.

However, Christian training requires more of us than simply dealing with sin. Later in Hebrews, another reference to athletic competition appears: "Let us throw off everything that hinders and the sin that so easily entangles, and let us run with perseverance the race marked out for us" (Heb. 12:1). Note the way the grammar frames the point: "Throw off everything that hinders *and* the sin that so easily entangles" (emphasis added). In other words, not everything that hinders us is sin.

It's not sinful for an athlete to eat an ice cream cone, but it may impede their ability to win the prize. Self-control is focused on the prize. Paul expressed it this way to the Philippian church: "*One thing I do: Forgetting what is behind and straining toward what is ahead, I press on toward the goal to win the prize for which God has called me heavenward in Christ Jesus*" (Phil. 3:13–14, emphasis added).

Do you see the connection with Peter's word for goodness—*areté*? As we saw in Chapter 4, to embody goodness means that we fulfill the unique potential entrusted to us. Self-control harnesses our minds and hearts on *one thing*, toward which we strain with all our energy.

Now, you may be expecting the challenge: Have you identified the *one thing* you were created to pursue, so important that you will sacrifice everything for it? And you may be thinking, this picture of an athlete competing at the highest level has little relation to the quiet routines that my life centers on.

The *one thing* Paul is exhorting us to pursue is not a destination. It's the journey that each of our distinctive lives takes.

Let me emphasize this point; it is the foundation for the book you're reading. I've already quoted the line from Kierkegaard's journal that inspired the title, *Becoming Yourself*: "And now, with God's help, I shall become myself." God doesn't want you to become Kierkegaard, or anyone else. He wants you to grow, with his help, into the unique person he created you to be, with your unique set of gifts and your unique circle of relationships and influence. We just read Hebrews 12:1, exhorting us to "run with perseverance the race marked out for us." Your race is different than mine, or anyone else's. The creation story in Genesis tells us that "God created man in his own image, in the image of God he created him; male and female he created them" (Genesis 1:27). You bear God's image in a unique way, and fulfilling that potential, running the race marked out for *you*, should be a central concern.

As I've reflected on my answer to this question of the *one thing*, it's occurred to me that my work at this stage of life is to assist several business and ministry leaders to pursue the mission God has assigned to them. My abilities, the resources I draw from my experience, and my opportunities for meaningful work have combined in this way. My roles are all secondary and behind the scenes. It seems right for this time of my life, and I'm content with it.

The life produced by self-control is rarely dramatic. It is not exemplified by the hero who, in a moment of crisis, takes a courageous stand or a great risk, whether that risk be financial, political, or military. Instead, *greatness is revealed in the person who expresses love in words and actions in the day-by-day routines of ordinary life.*

I quoted Proverbs 16:32 earlier: "Better a patient man than a warrior, a man who controls his temper than he who takes a city." A city is taken once; and the capture of a city can make a general's reputation for a lifetime. But controlling the tongue is a day-by-day discipline, marked not by grand gestures or large-scale accomplishments but by the quiet absence of commotion. It is not limited to the visionary or charismatic leader but is achievable by anyone who walks the path of obedience.

My son and daughter-in-law have two boys in elementary school. Every day, when they prepare lunch for the boys, they write a brief note and pack it in the lunchbox. A note is a small thing, but can you envision the power of hundreds of these notes on the boys' sense of love and security? This power accumulates gradually, day by day, through small but consistent effort, even on days when the parents are in a hurry or don't feel well. It's a picture of self-control in running their daily race. All of us have similar opportunities, though their application depends on factors unique to each of us.

Let me share a verse that forms a constant reminder for me. Ephesians 2:10 teaches that "we are God's workmanship, created in Christ Jesus to do good works, which God prepared in advance for us to do." I am haunted by the idea that God would bring someone to me who needs something I can provide, and instead I rationalize doing nothing—it's not my problem, it's not my responsibility, I'm busy with something else right now. When faced with what may feel like an interruption, rather than continuing with my program for the day, I try to exercise the self-control to stop, listen, and ask God for guidance in the moment.

I don't mean to imply that Christians cannot be visionary leaders. Certainly, there are Christian leaders whose expansive, far-seeing vision has led to great accomplishments. Some of them, based on what we know, seem to be paragons; others appear to lack the maturity or wisdom or character commensurate with their gifts. Often, we realize these deficiencies in retrospect when we see a leader implode, whether due to a moral failure or to being corrupted by success.

Sometimes God uses deeply flawed people to accomplish his purposes, although it doesn't always make sense that God would use a spiritually immature person to lead some great work. I wonder if it's because we harbor the wrong perspective on what "great work" consists of.

I have two friends, a married couple, who have spent more than thirty years in a small, obscure ministry in a Rust Belt city. They are gifted people who work harder than almost anyone I know. Some time ago, I was praying for them when the question occurred to me: Why do they serve in obscurity, while other ministry leaders achieve prominence despite having less talent, spiritual maturity, and diligence? Even more, why would God allow this couple to spend their lives in such a small ministry and never see the outsized results that come so easily for others?

I think God has placed my friends in that ministry, in that city, because he can trust them.

Each society has small subgroups where the gospel hasn't yet taken root. Some of these subgroups have been so mistreated by the prevailing culture that they reflexively mistrust any outsider. To present the Good News to them in a way that can be heard requires someone willing to devote a life to entering their culture and gaining their hard-won acceptance.

The people in these small subgroups are as important to God as anyone else.

It's easy to find leaders willing to take on ministries that are enjoyable, prestigious, and remunerative. But the prominence of the role has nothing to do with how God sees the value of the work. In contrast, leaders who faithfully serve a small, obscure group of people, and whose lifelong efforts achieve small results and provide small rewards—those kind of leaders are rare. I believe they are precious in God's eyes.

When we all stand before God, I have no doubt that the obscure servants who have spent a lifetime in seemingly unrewarded obedience will receive a greater reward than the person on the prominent ministry platform. This is what I think Jesus meant when he said, "So the last will be first, and the first will be last." (Matt. 20:16).

Just as the self-control of an athlete enables great power in the moment of competition, so the self-control Peter describes enables us to live powerfully, as we learn to draw on the power provided by God's Spirit day by day.

The word *power* evokes different mental images for different people. The way we think about power and what power means defines much of what is important to us.

During a coaching session with a young manager not long ago, after a lengthy discussion, I asked this question: "Do you think there is something inherently wrong with exercising power? Perhaps something, kind of dirty?" She looked at me with surprise, and after a thoughtful pause said, "Yes."

This viewpoint is widely held, and it stems from the experiences all of us have had with leaders and others who abused the power they exercised. Godly power is not abusive. Listen to Jesus' words to his disciples:

> "You know that the rulers of the Gentiles lord it over them, and their great men exercise authority over them. It is not this way among you, but whoever wishes to become great among you shall be your servant, and whoever wishes to be first among you shall be your slave; just as the Son of Man did not come to be served, but to serve, and to give His life a ransom for many." Matt. 20:25–28 (NASB)

I define godly power as a person's capacity to have an impact for good. A greater capacity for good is the outcome of a life of self-control. This kind of power is not solely the province of leaders. It is accessible to all of us as we draw on the power of the Spirit to run the race God has marked out for us with relentless perseverance. Paul exhorted his young protégé, Timothy, "For God did not give us a spirit of timidity, but a spirit of power, of love and of self-discipline" (2 Tim. 1:7).

I have learned that our ability to have an impact for good—our definition of Spirit-fueled power—depends on whether we have developed a moral authority that attracts support rather than provoking resistance. The power we exercise begins with our personal capacity and endurance, and it is either multiplied or diminished through the moral authority we exercise in relationships. Moral authority multiplies one's impact; it grows or diminishes based on the level of trust others place in us. When we demonstrate that we consistently act for the good of all rather than prioritizing our own good, others grant us moral authority.

This requires more than good intentions. First, we must be wise enough to recognize the good. To see clearly requires self-awareness and breadth of perspective. Second, we must have the capacity to translate our good intentions into positive actions, fueled by a pure love that enables us to look first to others' interests rather than our own.

Jesus challenged his disciples on precisely this point: "Who then is the faithful and wise servant, whom the master has put in charge of the servants in his household to give them their food at the proper time? It will be good for that servant whose master finds him doing so when he returns" (Matt. 24:45–46).

When I was in the process of acquiring the company that I led for many years, I was struck by the relationship of this passage to the responsibilities that loomed ahead. It struck me: this is how God sees my responsibility. I am responsible to "give food," to act for the good, for a small circle of people. And I remember thinking—this is true in every sphere of my life. I have a circle of relationships—overlapping circles of family, friends, church, neighbors, colleagues and co-workers, the work team I lead, and so forth—and I am responsible to act faithfully and considerately in the best interests of those in each circle. This is what it means to "give food" in my small corner of the world.

Wise enactment of self-control requires more than identifying our *one thing* and recognizing the temptations to sins, many of which are endemic to simply being human. We must also understand how our culture's values conflict with biblical teaching. Few concepts require more of an intellectual stretch than this one, because we are not accustomed to evaluating our cultural assumptions from the outside looking in.

Culture is like oxygen; it pervades our environment. Cultural values are often the things we take most for granted; they grow out of assumptions we have made without even realizing we have made them. Every culture is rooted in a set of shared assumptions.

As I noted earlier, the notion that everyone should be free to pursue life, liberty, and happiness in the way that seems best to them is so ingrained in American minds that it's difficult for us to imagine how anyone could think differently. If you have spent time in other cultural settings, it is likely that you've come to realize that this is not the only way to think.

Our culture provides our default settings. We are usually not aware of the cocoon in which we live, and to a greater or lesser extent we assume that our cultural values frame things in a way that is universally human rather than comprising only one of many possible ways to think. The fallacy of culture is that, like any human creation, it comprises a distorted lens through which we see. And culture is a fixed lens; it is always in place, whether we are aware of its presence or not.

Likewise, on a personal level, the habits and routines practiced in the home where you grew up will forever define what is "normal" for you. Those things you learned without realizing you were learning them—such as ways you observed your parents going about life when you were a small child—constitute "the way things should be" for you.

For example, my siblings and I never had pets in our home. My father had an aversion to the idea, an aversion that was often put into words after we had visited a family who had pets in their home. He couldn't understand why people would have pets. I've never understood it either; I have completely adopted my father's line of thinking, but I adopted it without realizing I was doing so. I now recognize that millions of happy pet owners are the norm and my view is abnormal. But the viewpoint ingrained in my childhood feels normal and rational to me.

I once heard an old pastor say that people tend to adopt their mother's theology. The answers small children receive from their earliest questions about the world around them—those which most often come from their mother if she is the parent who spends the most time in the home—become their bedrock assumptions, so deeply rooted that they are rarely the object of conscious thought. We are unlikely to question these assumptions unless circumstances force us to do so.

It follows, then, that culture wields its power through relationships. It's natural for us to adopt the assumptions shared by the people around us; this is how families work, and, with lesser intensity, it is how neighborhoods and communities work. We may have powerful motives to live in in alignment with our neighbors' approval, motives both internal to us (the desire for acceptance) and external (the desire to live in peace).

However, the Bible teaches that these motives can lead us to assign a high value to things not valued by God. Jesus challenged the Pharisees with these words: "How can you believe [in me] if you accept praise from one another, yet make no effort to obtain the praise that comes from the only God?" (John 5:44).

To run with the discipline of an athlete in the path that God marks out for us, we need to train our minds in different ways of thinking, informed by different sources. This requires that we seek out communities where what we learn can be clarified by wise fellow travelers and where we can be supported by those who share our values. This need is why the New Testament teaches that fellowship with other believers is essential for godly living.

A supportive, learning community is precisely what a church is intended to be, though I acknowledge that churches don't always live up to that standard. People have been hurt, misled, even betrayed or abused in a church setting. It can be hard to trust again for someone with that experience. And yet, if you don't think you need the church, you are unrealistic about yourself.

As we learn and are encouraged by the church, we can develop our ability to infuse what we have learned into our daily practices and habits. This happens as we discipline ourselves to act in accordance with those learnings. No one attains the power of living wisely and well without sustained hard work along the way.

This brings us back to putting aside those things that hinder us. As we have seen, sin is not the only source of hindrance. Even good things can hinder us in pursuit of the best—that *"one thing* I do" that Paul speaks of.

Gordon MacDonald once wrote that the challenge most followers of Christ face is not to refrain from egregious evil; rather, it's to select the best out of all the good-but-second-best things that compete for our time, energy, and attention.[14]

Of course, there isn't a list out there that ranks things in order of goodness. If only it were that simple! What is best for you may not be best for someone else with a different set of gifts or a different spiritual vocation. We learn to discern "the path marked out for us" through spiritual exploration, self-examination, and study of the Scriptures.

Does the name Winslow Homer ring a bell for you? Homer was a painter, a great one in my estimation. I suspect that were you to ask a panel of art historians who the greatest American painter of the nineteenth century was, Winslow Homer would get some votes.

In the early 1890s, Homer, his two brothers, and his brothers' families vacationed together on Prouts Neck, a rocky peninsula south of Portland, Maine. All of them loved the place, and they ended up buying a large waterfront home there. Homer's brothers used it as a summer home for their families, but Homer, who had never married, took the small carriage house, moved it about one hundred yards north to a spot where it had unobstructed ocean views, and hired an architect to turn it into a home and studio for him. The studio that was added onto the street side of the building was spacious, but the living area was tiny—no more than four hundred square feet.

I visited Homer's home and studio last year. It struck me that he kept virtually no possessions when he moved into his new home—a bench, a table and a couple of chairs, and a couch that he slept on. Why? He had plenty of money. But he had *one thing* he wanted to do for the rest of his life, so he structured his environment—his life—to exclude every distraction from that *one thing*, including superfluous possessions that he needed to care for.

Aged fifty-seven when he began to live in the repurposed carriage house, Homer lived another seventeen years, dying in this home at the age of seventy-four. Many of his greatest paintings are seascapes inspired by the view from his home and the rocky coastline below.

I resonate with Homer's desire to live with a minimum of possessions. I've simplified my life in recent years, admittedly not as ruthlessly as Homer did, but it has magnified my joy.

In contrast, I have a friend who devotes much of her time to maintaining an extensive piece of property that has been in her family for generations. It is a cherished place for her children and a wonderland for her young grandchildren. Providing an opportunity for ongoing family connection that is rooted in a place is meaningful to her and has the chance for an impact that will long outlive my friend. I see no reason to doubt that this is the best thing she could be doing.

What may serve as a hindrance for me may be an essential part of the path marked out for you. Each of us runs a different race. I'm enjoying freedom from possessions; my friend is maintaining possessions that may have an impact for generations. I think each of us is making the right choice, different though those choices are.

In addition to each of us having a different path, the best thing for us *today* may differ from what was best yesterday. We may need to leave cherished roles or ministries to free up time or other resources for a new task that God has put before us—pruning away last year's dead growth so new growth can take place.

Jesus' well-known metaphor of a vine and its branches expresses this truth about spiritual life. He said, "I am the true vine, and my Father is the gardener. He cuts off every branch in me that bears no fruit, while every branch that does bear fruit he prunes so that it will be even more fruitful" (John 15:1–2). And Jesus makes clear that fruitfulness is the goal: "This is to my Father's glory, that you bear much fruit" (John 15:8).

Self-control, then, should lead to fruitfulness. In fact, it reflects the kind of pruning Jesus speaks of, trimming away nonessential growth so that all the energy of the tree or vine is channeled into producing fruit. Producing the kind of fruit God desires to see in our lives reflects the ability to translate the knowledge that proceeds from faith into daily living.

Self-control is developed over time as we increase our ability to incorporate disciplines into daily living, and as we uncover where to apply discipline to produce spiritual fruit. We must learn to work against the grain of our desires, to sacrifice some things that are good and pleasing for the sake of the best. This is the price we must pay if, as Hebrews 12:1 expresses it, we are to "throw off everything that hinders and the sin that so easily entangles." The purpose is expressed in the rest of the verse: so we can "run with perseverance the race marked out for us."

Self-control frees us to focus our energies on the best things, but we must persevere if self-control is to take root. Let's look at perseverance next.

chapter seven

Perseverance

*. . . and to self-control, **perseverance** . . .*
2 PETER 1:6

not everyone finishes well. Some people fail spectacularly before they reach the finish line. Maybe it's a prominent politician whose moral failure is made public or a business leader who takes one risk too many. A dramatic fall may be triggered by an unwise decision or by the revelation of a dark secret.

Most often, though, a poor finish doesn't stem from a single disaster. Instead, people make repeated decisions that, over time, reveal that something is more important to them than God. Maybe it's comfort they seek; maybe money or power; maybe a hunger for prestige; or a source of pleasure or excitement that consumes more and more of their time and resources. In any case, when a desire for other things diminishes spiritual vitality, fruitfulness declines as well.

Just as the sudden fall of a seemingly healthy tree may be the outcome of a long period of internal decay, sudden disasters can be rooted in a long sequence of small and repeated decisions.

Jesus said that the way to destruction is broad, but the path of life is narrow, and few will find it. Many routes will take us off the right track. Furthermore, there exists a creative, determined enemy of our souls.

Tolstoy begins *Anna Karenina* with these apt words: "Happy families are all alike; but unhappy families are each unhappy in their own way." There are ways of life that can seem more interesting, exciting, and challenging than the bland domesticity we often associate with simple family life, but they often lead to grief.

Perseverance consists of steadily walking a path of daily obedience and faithfulness—obedience to God and faithfulness in our relationships and responsibilities. Much of this chapter will focus specifically on persevering through suffering. In my experience and that of many other followers of Christ, suffering produces the distinctive test of faith and the temptation to give up. However, seeking fulfillment in the day-to-day routines of ordinary life when our relationships seem dull and our work unfulfilling requires perseverance as well. Suffering can knock us off track; lack of joy can cause us to drift off course, often gradually; the result is the same either way.

James begins his eponymous letter with these words:

Consider it pure joy, my brothers, whenever you face trials of many kinds, because you know that the testing of your faith develops perseverance. Perseverance must finish its work so that you may be mature and complete, not lacking anything. (Jas. 1:2–4)

Notice what James says about perseverance: if you possess it, you are "mature and complete, not lacking anything." Does this mean that perseverance is the capstone of the qualities of character? Perseverance, like knowledge, is an instrumental quality; when we embody perseverance, it shows we have the capacity to embody the other qualities too. As we walk the daily path of obedience and faithfulness, we embed love, faith, godliness, and goodness more deeply in our character. Of course, all the character qualities are interrelated; each of them is supported by the others.

For example, you cannot persevere long without having faith, without the belief that your striving has meaning and importance. Paul exhorted the Corinthian church, ". . . stand firm. Let nothing move you. Always give yourselves fully to the work of the Lord, *because you know that your labor in the Lord is not in vain.*" (1 Cor. 15:58, emphasis added). We can be steadfast during a test of faith because we believe that our work for the Lord has eternal value. In fact, as James says, it is distinctively the "testing of your faith" that develops perseverance.

It takes more than faith, though, to maintain your course in the face of discouragement, difficulties, and suffering. Discouragement can be paralyzing. Even when we are confident that our difficult path is the right one, our capacity to persevere in acting rightly is not ensured. In addition to faith, then, perseverance builds upon self-control. Putting one foot in front of another when you're discouraged requires that you have developed the habit of doing so.

In the same way, perseverance builds on knowledge. As we have seen, the knowledge that Peter exhorts us to grasp enables us to live wisely and powerfully in the moment, armed with the knowledge that God's purpose for us cannot be thwarted, and that nothing can separate us from his enduring, unshakable love. This knowledge helps us discern the path that is marked out for us and produces maturity as we walk in it.

Perseverance builds on all these qualities. And these other qualities are expressed most fully as we develop the capacity to persevere.

The Scriptures emphasize again and again that perseverance will bring fulfillment:

- So do not throw away your confidence; it will be richly rewarded. You need to persevere so that when you have done the will of God, you will receive what he has promised. (Heb. 10:35–36)
- Let us not become weary in doing good, for at the proper time we will reap a harvest if we do not give up. (Gal. 6:9)
- I, John, your brother and companion in the suffering and kingdom and patient endurance that are ours in Jesus . . . (Rev. 1:9)
- Be faithful, even to the point of death, and I will give you the crown of life. (Rev. 2:10)
- We also rejoice in our sufferings, because we know that suffering produces perseverance; perseverance, character; and character, hope. And hope does not disappoint us. (Rom. 5:3-5)

Notice how often suffering is paired with perseverance in the verses just quoted. Perseverance is the quality that enables us to earn the reward, but it comes through experience that can shipwreck us: the experience of suffering.

Paul puts it bluntly in Romans 5:3 "Suffering produces perseverance." Likewise, James says it's the testing of our faith that produces perseverance, specifically the trials we endure. In Revelation 1:9, John links these ideas together: "the suffering and kingdom and patient endurance"—suffering, perseverance, and then the reward.

My study of the Bible's teaching, my personal experience, and what I have learned from people whose lives I've shared, all point to the same conclusion: *suffering is the primary method that God uses to mature us.* It uniquely tests our faith, because it forces us to face the truth about what we believe—and specifically, what we believe about God.

In Chapter 3, we talked about the test of faith and how it confronts us with these questions: Do we still believe that God is good? Do we believe he cares about us? Do we retain our confidence that nothing can separate us from him? Do we believe that our suffering will bring about good in our lives (Rom. 8:28)?

The test of faith always comes down to one question: Do I believe the truth about God? The pressure of suffering can distort our picture of God and affect how we answer. We may be tempted, in anger or despair, to believe a lie such as, surely God doesn't love me if he allows this to happen, or, God can't be good if he allows evil to flourish in our world.

Suffering does not produce growth automatically; we must respond to it rightly. We must accept that God is allowing us to suffer for a good purpose of his. We must say yes to the process, rather than growing angry, resentful, or bitter.

Hebrews 10:35–36, one of the passages listed above, contains the promise of a rich reward for those who persevere. Here is the rest of that passage: "For in just a very little while, 'he who is coming will come and will not delay. But my righteous one will live by faith. And if he shrinks back, I will not be pleased with him'" (Heb. 10:37–38). When the test comes, bringing suffering in its wake, we need to keep walking the path God has marked out for us—straight through. We must not shrink back.

If we are to persevere through difficult times, our faith must be more than a rootless set of feelings. Nor are clearly framed theological beliefs enough. Most of all, our lives must embody what we believe. Faith must be established in our lives through disciplines that enable us to respond rightly under pressure.

Nassim Nicholas Taleb is best known for his book *The Black Swan* about the impact of outsized, unforeseeable, and era-changing events that have occurred throughout history. In a subsequent book titled

Antifragile, Taleb focuses primarily on institutions, which he classifies as fragile, resilient, or anti-fragile. A fragile institution is brittle and easily damaged; Taleb's prime example is a bank, which is perpetually vulnerable to stresses from a wide range of predictable sources, and whose high level of debt to depositors magnifies the impact of those stresses. An authoritarian government is also fragile; once its repressive authority is breached, total collapse often follows.

When I think about resilience, the second category, I picture a new home or commercial building in my hometown of Charleston, South Carolina. Charleston lies in the Atlantic hurricane belt, and the construction of new buildings is governed by strict building codes. The goal of these codes is that new structures are designed and built to withstand a powerful storm.

In the thirty years that I have lived in Charleston, my homes have endured several storms and yet sustained only minor damage. I've seen the building codes serve the purpose for which they were devised. However, even a well-built home cannot repair itself. Damage may be minimized and a home's contents protected, but the home is certainly not stronger *after* the storm than it was before.

A living person is different.

Take the example of strength training. By engaging our muscles with resistance, we make them stronger. Training with heavy weights not only strengthens muscles but also helps our bodies shift nutrients to strengthen our bones. As we train with heavier weights, over time we increase our strength in proportion to the resistance we overcome. This is how Taleb defines anti-fragile: an institution or person with the capacity to grow stronger as it faces resistance.

It is the same for a follower of Christ who develops the capacity to persevere in the face of trials. Trials present resistance in our lives like weights present resistance to our muscles. As we persevere through trials, we strengthen our faith, which in turn increases our capacity to persevere through even more difficult trials ahead. Through this process, we can learn to rely more steadily and draw more readily on the resources of the Spirit living within us. This is the essence of character as we've defined it: Character comprises the resources you possess for responding to life's challenges and its opportunities.

As we develop perseverance, we cease to be fragile and unstable, but "he who doubts is like a wave of the sea, blown and tossed by the wind" (Jas. 1:6).

We go beyond resilience, which weathers stronger storms but not without damage.

Those who persevere have learned to use trials, losses, and defeats to become stronger than before. They can say of themselves as Paul said, near the end of his life, "I can do all things through Christ who strengthens me" (Phil. 4:13, NKJV).

But we must also realize that perseverance is not necessarily rewarded by success. When it is, we celebrate those stories. And we remind each other that it's always darkest before dawn, so we don't give in just before we might see victory. But we also need to realize that victory is not always in the cards. Perseverance doesn't always produce a happy ending. As I mentioned in the chapter on faith, I persevered in attempting to save my glass company, but my efforts weren't successful, and I still have a sense of loss from the experience of having to close and liquidate the business.

Hebrews 11 commemorates many heroes of faith; the chapter closes with this observation: "These were all commended for their faith, *yet none of them received what had been promised*" (Heb. 11:39, emphasis added).

Galatians 6:9 exhorts us, "Let us not become weary in doing good, for at the proper time we will reap a harvest if we do not give up." But "the proper time" may not be in our lifetimes, or in this world. We persevere by faith; "we fix our eyes not on what is seen, but on what is unseen" (2 Cor. 4:18).

I find it daunting to think about the kinds of crises that require long-term perseverance. But when God says, "Never will I leave you; never will I forsake you" (Heb. 13:5), he means it. We never face the test of faith alone.

His admonition to Joshua applies to us also: "Do not be terrified; do not be discouraged, for the Lord your God will be with you wherever you go" (Josh. 1:9). When we face the test of faith, we can also experience the faithfulness of God.

I've spent many years working in manufacturing environments. One of the primary goals in production is to replicate each process with near perfect consistency. When the customer opens their box of corn flakes at the breakfast table, you don't want them to be surprised at what they find.

In an earlier chapter, we reviewed the difference between education and training. Education—simply knowing the correct process—has very little to do with consistency. What's needed is training: repetitive practice so that consistency becomes automatic.

We saw earlier how the military trains recruits. They don't merely explain what to do in dangerous situations; they train young soldiers how to respond. When danger comes, the soldier won't be relaxed or have the leisure to ponder what to do. Instead, as waves of adrenaline surge through the soldier's body, fueling powerful fight-or-flight responses, they will simply *act*. It's impossible to think calmly and judiciously about the right response in those moments. One's *only* chance to respond well, and perhaps to survive, is if the right response has become automatic— something the soldier doesn't have to think about or even choose.

The same is true in times of spiritual stress.

The time-honored purpose of spiritual disciplines such as prayer, Bible study, and meditation is to enable us to become practiced in the right responses so that responding well under pressure comes naturally.

This also applies to life disciplines such as commitment, cultivating a responsive heart, seeking accountability, and working for justice. The writer of Hebrews urges his readers to "leave the elementary teachings about Christ and go on to maturity" (Heb. 6:1). The mature are those "who by constant use have trained themselves to distinguish good from evil" (Heb. 5:14). Young Christians learn the teachings, but maturity develops from training—disciplines that are reinforced again and again through "constant use."

We must often distinguish good from evil in the moment, amid ambiguity or lack of information. We may be pressured to accept or condone that which isn't good. Training is essential if we are to please God by our obedience in the pressure of the moment.

The other purpose of training is to produce fitness. Vince Lombardi famously said, "Fatigue makes cowards of us all." Our capacity to persevere must be developed systematically if we are to achieve our potential in its performance. In the chapter on self-control, we reviewed how Hebrews 12 uses an extended metaphor of competitive running to evoke a picture of the way we are to live. In Hebrews 12:1, we read, "Run with perseverance the race marked out for us."

We are urged to remember the opposition Jesus endured so we will not grow weary and lose heart, and we are told, "Endure hardship as discipline" (Heb. 12:7). The difficulties we undergo, whether external opposition or the challenge of quenching our own sinfulness, are part of the training discipline that builds our capacity to endure.

Yet more than simply enduring, the goal is to emerge stronger on the other side.

And as we persevere through the test of faith, we are increasingly shaped in the Lord's likeness. In other words, we grow in godliness. Let's talk about this quality next.

chapter eight

Godliness

> *His divine power has given us everything we need*
> *for **life** and **godliness** through our knowledge of him*
> *who called us by his own glory and goodness*
>
> *. . . and to perseverance, **godliness** . . .*
>
> 2 PETER 1:3, 6

or much of my life, the word *godliness* felt off-putting to me. I pictured an existence drained of life, defined by denial and abstention. That's not what Peter means at all. Consider how he connects "life" and "godliness" in verse 3 of our passage above. By pairing these two words, Peter means to convey quite the opposite of denial and abstention.

The Greek word translated as "life" in this verse is *zoe*, which signifies vitality, animation, and fullness of life. In contrast, the other Greek word often translated as "life" is *bios*. As you might guess from the English words that come from it, *bios* refers to the living, breathing, creaturely functions of an organism.

Peter is telling us that godliness exudes vitality. A godly person possesses energy and joy that combine to produce a rich, full life. Following Christ does not narrow our lives. Rather, it broadens our lives immeasurably, opening us to extraordinary possibilities. Jesus said, "I have come that they may have life, and have it to the full" (John 10:10). It's life in this exact sense that Peter writes about.

Another common misconception is that godliness describes smug, self-righteous people who create rules for so-called "right living" and then preen themselves on their compliance with their rules. I have seen people who earnestly seek to practice godliness still end up in that place. Intent on parsing the difference between the choices they face, over time they come to assign supreme importance to relatively minor distinctions. In doing this, they miss the point of godliness altogether.

Godliness is much more than good deeds. One of Jesus' jarring statements about life is this: "Unless your righteousness surpasses that of the Pharisees and the teachers of the law, you will certainly not enter the kingdom of heaven" (Matt. 5:20). This statement must have shocked his disciples. As we noted earlier, the Pharisees were notably strict—even ostentatiously so—in their performance of the Law's requirements. If righteousness is measured by the performance of religious actions, then it would be hard to win a righteousness contest with a Pharisee.

Jesus wanted his disciples to understand that external compliance with religious rules is not sufficient to gain entrance to the kingdom of heaven. Following him requires more than acts of obedience; it requires sincerity of heart. He went on to provide examples of what he meant, and here is perhaps the best-known example: "You have heard that it was said, 'Do not commit adultery.' But I tell you that anyone who looks at a woman lustfully has already committed adultery with her in his heart" (Matt. 5:27–28).

Sinful attitudes overlaid with a veneer of righteous actions do not constitute godliness in the sense that Jesus meant; nor is that what

Peter intended. Godliness may be revealed by our actions, but it goes much further. As with other dimensions of character, it isn't the façade we present to the world but what we embody that counts—what flows out from us.

Another metaphor describing the internal dimensions of godliness is provided in Hebrews 5:13–14, a passage we have touched on in several contexts: "Anyone who lives on milk, being still an infant, is not acquainted with the teaching about righteousness. But solid food is for the mature, who by constant use have trained themselves to distinguish good from evil." Note that the focus is on *distinguishing* good from evil rather than on *doing* good. This passage is speaking not of good actions but of the progress in discernment that we usually call wisdom.

Another way to say this is that *godliness is a matter of the spirit that infuses a person.* Godliness does not define itself by what it abstains from but by what it chooses. A godly person distinguishes good from evil to choose the good—those things that enrich life and relationships. It's in line with the way Paul uses the Greek word *areté* ("goodness") in Philippians 4:8, which we considered earlier. The spirit of a godly person chooses "whatever is true, whatever is noble, whatever is right, whatever is pure, whatever is lovely, whatever is admirable" (Phil. 4:8).

The other day a young pastor commented to me that he struggles with this teaching from the book of James: "Everyone should be quick to listen, slow to speak" (Jas. 1:19). He struggles sometimes to refrain from jumping into a conversation when someone else is speaking, and he wanted to know how to manage that urge to speak.

As he and I talked, I suggested that he had missed James's point. The young pastor was trying to discipline himself to restrain his flow of words; in contrast, James was describing a posture or approach toward other people.

If I care about a friend, co-worker, or neighbor, I am naturally eager to listen, to draw out their thinking or feelings so I can better understand.

We listen so that our "love may abound more and more in knowledge and depth of insight" (Phil. 1:9). If we care deeply for another person, wanting to listen to them will be as natural as wanting to speak. We will want to know the one we love, just as we want to be known by them.

Far from embodying a bloodless sanctity, godliness is an animating force. It lives in us when we are infused with a worshipful spirit and when our own impulses are rooted in and nourished by reverence to Christ.

Godliness is the vital life force that produces that fruit of goodness, righteousness, and truth in each one of us. Jesus said, "Every good tree bears good fruit, but a bad tree bears bad fruit. A good tree cannot bear bad fruit, and a bad tree cannot bear good fruit. Every tree that does not bear good fruit is cut down and thrown into the fire. Thus, by their fruit you will recognize them" (Matt. 7:17–20). The degree to which we embody godliness determines whether the fruit we produce is good.

You may be able to fake godliness for a time, but eventually the quality of the fruit your life produces will become apparent to those around you.

False godliness is what Jesus condemned when he said that our righteousness must surpass that of the Pharisees, who wrapped themselves in a mantle of good actions to cover stained and knotted hearts.

Paul paints a stark picture of false godliness in 2 Timothy 3: "There will be terrible times in the last days. People will be lovers of themselves, lovers of money, boastful, proud, abusive, disobedient to their parents, ungrateful, unholy, without love, unforgiving, slanderous, without self-control, brutal, not lovers of the good, treacherous, rash, conceited, lovers of pleasure rather than lovers of God" (2 Tim. 3:1–4). Paul ends this litany of sinful behavior with an unexpected twist: "having a form of godliness but denying its power" (2 Tim. 3:5).

As we read Paul's description of the last days, it may sound as though Paul is speaking about those outside the church who oppose God's people and persecute them. Yet verse 5 makes it plain that Paul is talking about the church itself. Terrible times are ahead, not because the church is under attack from its enemies, but because it is undermined by members of the body who think godliness is only a matter of the surface and not a matter of the heart.

It may seem an overstatement to warn that terrible times are in store for us because some strike a righteous pose. Why would Paul say this? He saw that "having a form of godliness" but not the real thing would rot a church from within. Many religions have taught that pleasing the gods is a matter of performing certain ritual actions to placate them. It doesn't matter what you think about the rituals you perform; external compliance is all that matters.

Christianity (and Judaism for that matter) is different. As God explained to Samuel when he was about to anoint David as Israel's future king, "The Lord does not look at the things man looks at. Man looks at the outward appearance, but the Lord looks at the heart" (1 Sam. 16:7). And, in the Lord's eyes, as Paul wrote, "The only thing that counts is faith expressing itself through love" (Gal. 5:6).

There are many ways in which these terrible times have been evidenced in my own lifetime. The church has been influenced by the celebrity culture that surrounds it. People are drawn to larger-than-life personalities like moths to a bright porch light. The result is that the leaders of many large congregations are more noteworthy for their glittering gifts than for rooted godliness.

With great success comes great temptation. I think most anyone who has experienced a measure of success, no matter in what arena, would agree. I have also seen that spiritual vulnerability is heightened by success, and many prominent leaders succumb. The Christian leader whose "fall from grace" first comes to mind for you will undoubtedly depend on your age or church affiliation, but each generation has far too many painful examples.

Our world is full of congregations thronged by affluent people who focus more on being served than on serving others. They lavish millions on beautiful facilities for weekly gatherings, gatherings that are pleasant, interesting, and comfortable. Yet they challenge no one to get out of their cushy seats and lay down their lives to work for justice, care for the fatherless, or serve the poor. The clothes they wear, words they use, and rituals they invoke all carry with them only a "form of godliness." A fake.

My favorite of Søren Kierkegaard's works is a discourse titled *Purity of Heart Is to Will One Thing*. I have returned to it again and again. The book takes as its starting point two passages from the book of James:

> If any of you lacks wisdom, he should ask God, who gives generously to all without finding fault, and it will be given to him. But when he asks, he must believe and not doubt, because he who doubts is like a wave of the sea, blown and tossed by the wind. That man should not think he will receive anything from the Lord; he is a double-minded man, unstable in all he does. (James 1:5–8)

> Submit yourselves, then, to God. Resist the devil, and he will flee from you. Come near to God and he will come near to you. Wash your hands, you sinners, and purify your hearts, you double-minded. (James 4:7-8)

Note that both passages focus on the person who is double-minded. What does it mean to be double-minded? *The life of a double-minded person hosts competing loves.* While double-minded people seek the good, they want other things at the same time. A person who wavers between incompatible desires can be neither strong nor stable. Those who are double-minded cannot be consistent in any direction or wholehearted in any stand they make.

One of the foundational teachings in evangelical Christian culture is the notion that all of us, to be spiritually and emotionally healthy, must live within a community. We are urged to "do life together" with our brothers and sisters as each of us walks the path that God has marked out for us.

As we have seen, there is no doubt that community is intended by God for our good and is necessary for us to live as whole and complete persons. Yet there is also a danger to our souls that is inherent when we think of ourselves as part of a group.

Most people are reluctant to take a stance that puts them at odds with the majority. We find it is easier to be silent, even when a group supports a position that we believe to be wrong. And when the majority holds a belief that differs from our own thinking, we may even change our beliefs to be accepted.

This tendency is illustrated by an experiment I participated in many years ago. The liberal arts college that I attended had a large psychology department. My fellow students frequently asked me to participate in lab experiments required for their coursework.

One evening, I walked down to the psych building to oblige a friend. Once I arrived, he asked me to sit in a chair, then told me that I would be asked math questions. If the answer I gave was correct, a green light would flash directly in front of me; if my answer was incorrect, a red light would flash instead.

I can do math problems in my head all day long. When I am tempted to think highly of this gift, I remind myself that it can easily be replicated by a five-dollar calculator. Nonetheless, I am confident in my ability to add, subtract, multiply, and divide.

As my friend began to ask questions, every answer I gave triggered a red light. Every answer. Initially, I was surprised. I answered subsequent questions with greater care, yet I still saw a red light each time. After this sequence was repeated several times, I decided to give an incorrect answer. I was immediately rewarded with a green light.

So I gave a second wrong answer and saw another green light. It's probably of no surprise that when I started answering questions correctly again, the red light flashed every time.

At that point, I said to my friend conducting the lab, "Hey, I know what you're doing. You're giving red lights for correct answers and green lights for wrong answers. I can sit here all night long if you want to, but I'm not going to give wrong answers."

He smiled and said, "Thanks, that's all I need this evening." As I left the room, he gave me a debrief paper to explain what the lab experiment was designed to test.

I read the debrief paper with interest as I walked back to my dorm. As it turned out, the purpose of the experiment that night was to determine what people would choose if they had to decide between being correct or being affirmed. The hypothesis that the experiment was designed to test was that most people would choose to be affirmed, even if they knew the affirmation was wrongly given.

This experiment depicts one of the enduring characteristics of human beings: that our sense of right and wrong is more malleable than we tend to think. We are more likely to go along with a crowd, even when we know it's heading in the wrong direction, than we are to go in the right direction if we must walk alone.

Furthermore, when we recognize sin in ourselves, it's both easy and comforting to compare ourselves to others. We might think we are better than the people around us; or we may rationalize a dubious activity or pattern of thought by how common it is among our peers.

We all know that culturally accepted standards of behavior have shifted in recent decades for garden-variety vices like public profanity, extramarital sex, and drug and alcohol consumption; I think we would agree that standards have shifted within the church as well. I realize that church standards fifty years ago were just as culturally influenced as they are today; the fact that we see an issue differently does not necessarily mean that we are ignoring biblical teaching. However, the distance we have moved in accepting formerly unacceptable behavior seems far beyond what the unchanging biblical standard warrants.

The issue is that we are double-minded. We would like to obey God, but we want to fit comfortably within our culture also.

We tend to second-guess ourselves when we realize others hold opinions that differ from our own. To an extent, this self-questioning is a good thing. We are all fallible; we all have gaps in our knowledge and should consider the possibility that others may have better information or better insight; and we are all blind to the ways in which our biases and unexamined assumptions lead to misunderstanding and false conclusions.

We are not obliged to have wise opinions about matters that are beyond our understanding. However, there are certain decisions that are required of us. When we make these decisions, we must not waver, regardless of how many people are arrayed in opposition.

Kierkegaard asks us, "Do you press yourself into the crowd, where the one excuses himself with the others, where at one moment there are, so to speak, many, and where in the next moment, each time that the talk touches on responsibility, there is no one? . . . In eternity, you will not be asked inquisitively and professionally, as though by a newspaper reporter, whether there were many that had the same—wrong opinion. You will be asked only whether you have held it."[15]

In our culture infused with democratic values, numbers are important. The majority rules. As Kierkegaard notes, "Eternity, on the other hand, never counts. The individual is always only one and conscience in its meticulous way concerns itself with the individual."[16]

We need to live our day-to-day lives with our eternal destination in mind. Stated another way, *we cannot hide within a crowd.* Nor can we comfort ourselves with the knowledge that, if we're mistaken, we'll have much company. "Wide is the gate and broad is the road that leads to destruction, and many enter through it" (Matt. 7:13).

Godliness does not consist in our ability to stand alone. However, standing alone may sometimes be required of us. Godliness is as crucial in its own way as perseverance if we are to lead fruitful lives. Without the animating energy that a single-hearted love for God produces, walking the path of faith can be exhausting. Discipline can only take us so far. But perseverance fueled by godliness is not a slog; it is a race we run with strength, confidence, and joy.

Psalm 1 draws a picture of the godly life, envisioning it as "a tree planted by streams of water" (v. 3). This metaphor recalls what Jesus said to the Samaritan woman at the well: "Whoever drinks the water I give him will never thirst. Indeed, the water I give him will become in him a spring of water welling up to eternal life" (John 4:14). Plainly Jesus is not talking about biological life; the word he uses is *zoe*, not *bios. Zoe* refers to a spiritual life that is rich, full, abundantly vital, and deeply connected to God.

Psalm 1 provides several insights into how we can embody this godly vitality.

First, a godly person is careful about the company he keeps. The psalm begins, "Blessed is the man who does not walk in the counsel of the wicked or stand in the way of sinners or sit in the seat of mockers." As we have seen, even the church can nurture double-mindedness, but its purpose is to build us up in faith and godliness. We are exhorted,

"Let us not give up meeting together, as some are in the habit of doing, but let us encourage one another" (Heb. 10:25). The encouragement of like-minded fellow runners as we run our respective races is powerful and needed.

Second, the Bible provides the corrective to the sometimes-errant voice of the crowd. Psalm 1 tells us of the godly person, "His delight is in the law of the Lord, and on his law he meditates day and night" (v. 2). The Bible provides a lens through which we are to view all of life, and it should inform how we understand and respond to what we see. This is not a burden; it is where a godly person finds their delight. The closest we can approach to the mind of God is to meditate day and night on what he has revealed to us.

Finally, the psalmist reminds us that we live in God's presence and within his care: "The Lord watches over the way of the righteous" (v. 6). We can trust in the faithfulness of God to develop in us the godliness that he desires to see.

Faith, goodness, knowledge, self-control, perseverance, godliness— all these qualities combine to produce the joyful, fruitful maturity that pleases God. Love is the most powerful quality of all. It is next on Peter's list; let's examine what that means for us.

chapter nine

Brotherly Kindness and Love

> *. . . and to godliness, **brotherly kindness**;*
> *and to brotherly kindness, **love**.*
>
> 2 PETER 1:7

s we have seen, the qualities Peter urges us to increase interact with and overlap with each other—none stands in isolation from the others. Together, they resemble a bowl of oatmeal rather than a bowl of marbles.

However, I believe it is significant that the list begins with faith; all the qualities are rooted in faith. "Without faith it is impossible to please God" (Heb. 11:6). When we accept God's gift of salvation by faith, his Spirit enters our lives. As God's Spirit works in us and through us, growth becomes possible in every dimension of life.

I also believe it is significant that Peter's list of qualities ends with love. All the other qualities find their fulfillment in love. One of the best-known passages on love begins with these words:

If I speak in the tongues of men and of angels, but have not love, I am only a resounding gong or clanging cymbal. If I have the gift of prophecy and can fathom all mysteries and all knowledge, and if I have a faith that can move mountains, but have not love, I am nothing. If I give all I possess to the poor and surrender my body to the flames, but have not love, I gain nothing. (1 Corinthians 13:1–3)

It doesn't matter how good you are, how much knowledge you have, or how much self-control you bring to bear *unless these virtues are rooted in and infused with love.*

Brotherly kindness and love are the two qualities that bring Peter's list to completion. Let's examine them together. Brotherly kindness and love are inseparable and likewise complementary. We lose important insights if we consider them as distinct concepts with differing implications.

I suspect that these two words held special resonance for Peter. Both words were prominent in his last conversation with Jesus, recorded in John 21. This encounter occurs after the resurrection, and the gospels give several indications that Peter is grieving, having denied three times that he even knew Jesus the night he was betrayed. Jesus uses this conversation to affirm Peter and restore him to ministry.

Peter and several other disciples had just spent all night fishing on the Sea of Galilee but hadn't caught a thing. As morning dawned, a man called to them from the shore. He told them to cast their nets on the other side of the boat. The resulting catch was so great that they couldn't haul it all in. In that moment, they realized that it was Jesus who had called out to them, and they quickly brought their boats ashore.

Jesus was already preparing a meal for them. After everyone ate, Jesus asked Peter, while no doubt motioning to the other disciples, "Simon son of John, do you truly love me more than these?" (John 21:15). Here, Jesus used the Greek word *agápē*, which denotes a selfless love.

Peter responded, "Yes, Lord, you know that I love you." However, Peter responds with a different word for "love"—*philéo*, which was more often used to denote familial love.

Some biblical commentators draw a specific inference from Peter's use of a different word in his response than the one Jesus used in his question. In their view, Jesus asked, "Peter, are you willing to lay down your life for me?" to which Peter, in effect, responded, "Well, Lord, you know I like you a lot."

Jesus asked the same question a second time, and Peter responded in the same way. However, when Jesus questioned Peter a third time, Jesus also used the word *philéo*. Many commentators interpret this change to mean that Jesus finally asked him, "Peter, do you even like me?" In this perspective, *agápē* reflects the highest form of love, while *philéo* is an inferior version, presumably for the less committed or less spiritually mature.

A different sense of the meaning of these words emerges when you look more broadly at how *agápē* and *philéo* are used in the New Testament. In fact, they are often used interchangeably. For example, in the post-resurrection chapters in John, both words are used to describe Jesus' love for John himself:

- ". . . the other disciple, the one Jesus loved [philéo]" (John 20:2)
- "The disciple whom Jesus loved [agápē] said to Peter . . ." (John 21:7)

If Jesus' love for John is described using both words, and within a few paragraphs of his interchange with Peter, presumably, then, *philéo* is not considered an inferior version of love that passes away when one is capable of *agápē*. Instead, the two words are better seen as complementary aspects of love within a relationship. Jesus affirms Peter's *philéo* love for him while calling him to reach beyond it to *agápē*. Let's explore what we can learn from Peter's pairing of these two words.

Agápē refers to a love that is distinctively Christian. In fact, *agápē* is arguably the most distinctive feature in Christian teaching, a revolutionary feature that separates it from the religions that had come before. *Agápē* is how we love others who are different from us or are our enemies or even unknown to us.

Because we become loving people when we are filled with God's Spirit and are thereby empowered to live lives full of love, we can "*agápē*" even someone who is unlovable, just as Christ loved us and gave himself for us while we were still separated from God by sin (Rom. 5:8; Eph. 5:2). *Agápē* denotes an act of will or purpose, not merely affection.

However, this does not replace the love that we carry for our families, whether we think of the siblings we grew up with in our childhood homes or of the brothers and sisters in Christ with whom we are growing in God's church. This kind of love remains important and is not superseded by growing maturity. Every human culture places a high value on family ties.

In 2 Peter 1:7, the word translated as "brotherly kindness" is *philadelphia*, a word that combines the word *philéo* (which means "to love") with the the word *adelphós* (which denotes "brother" or near relative). This compound word points to the family-like relationships that should characterize the community of believers. After all, it's natural to express love differently in different relationships. Perhaps, then, Peter's use of the word *agápē* in the same verse is intended to emphasize that we should love non-Christians as well.

Paul wrote, "Therefore, as we have opportunity, let us do good to all people, especially to those who belong to the family of believers" (Gal. 6:10). We are to love everyone, whether they be inside or outside of the church, but we have a special responsibility to serve our family of fellow believers.

A seemingly universal aspect of human behavior is the tendency to categorize others either as "one of us" or "one of them." At every level of human society, the distinction between us and them has taken place. Throughout much of human history, "one of us" was defined as the immediate and extended family or clan. You could argue that the growth and stability of civilized communities has been a direct function of its citizens' abilities to expand their definition of *us*.

In fact, an inclusive definition of *us* is necessary if we are to live in peace with our neighbors. In contrast, the bigotries that our society's values have taught us to deplore, such as racism and sexism, stem from the practice of using these differences to classify others as *them*.

God loves everyone, and Christians are meant to love in the very same way. In Luke 10, Jesus teaches us that *loving God and loving our neighbors is the greatest commandment* (v. 25–27). He told his listeners, "Do this and you will live" (v. 28). When one of his listeners asked in response, "And who is my neighbor?" (v. 29), Jesus answered by telling the well-known parable of the Good Samaritan (vv. 30–37).

The phrase *Good Samaritan* is so familiar to us that it's hard to grasp the way that Samaritans were reviled by the Jews in Jesus' day. It would have been extremely provocative to teach those Jews about loving their neighbors as themselves, as the Law commanded (Lev. 19:18), by telling a story that centers on a Samaritan.

Agápē, then, this inclusive love for the "other," complements and extends, rather than replaces, the human love for family that comes more naturally to us.

While *agápē* is always spoken of in Scripture as pure, holy, and high-minded, striving after *agápē* can be corrupted as with any human endeavor. Our sense that we embody *agápē* can sometimes be illusory.

If you have worked for a ministry or nonprofit organization that's designed to meet basic human needs, you know that even the process of generous giving can be corrupted. Those who have resources to share often fall into a benefactor-supplicant relationship with those who are in need. Supplicants soon learn that their willingness to adapt to what the benefactor wants, their ability to say the words that the benefactor likes to hear—maybe even their ability to convey the sense that they are one of the "deserving poor"—can all influence whether they receive their share of the resources that are doled out.

The imbalance of power and resources makes this kind of relationship inherently faulty and unequal. When a person in need—let's say a mother with hungry children—sees she can assure her family is fed if she offers lavish thanks, who can blame her if she does so? And when a benefactor who is trying to do good is flattered with the notion that he is both skillful and noble, it is easy for that benefactor to believe it.

Do you see how a desire to express *agápē* can be distorted? But blending *agápē* with brotherly kindness can equalize those relationships.

I am one of six children. As we grew up together, differences emerged in our abilities and interests, but my brothers and sisters and I know that we are equals. We come from the same place, we learned the same values from the same set of parents, and we developed many similar assumptions through our shared experiences. Though we acknowledge each other's gifts, we know each other too well to be impressed by one another, and we share a bond of relationship that has existed for every moment of our lives.

Agápē and *philéo* express complementary dimensions of love, then, and both are needed. *Agápē* forms the basis for a self-giving way of life, while *philéo* expresses the way we cherish, and treat as equals, the specific individuals whom we know and love.

It can be easier to love our brothers and sisters—those who look like us and have been shaped by the same experiences—than to love those people whom we view as different. Yet Christ teaches that we are to love all our neighbors, whether they share a family resemblance or not.

In Chapter 5, we examined words from Paul's letter to the Philippian church, a group of people who had consistently and sacrificially supported his work for years and whom he deeply loved: "And this is my prayer: that your love may abound more and more in knowledge and depth of insight, so that you may be able to discern what is best and may be pure and blameless until the day of Christ, filled with the fruit of righteousness that comes through Jesus Christ" (Phil. 1:9–11).

As we saw, we don't tend to pair love with "knowledge and depth of insight." We think of love as subjective rather than objective, rooted in feelings rather than knowledge. We think we must adopt an attitude of distance and impartiality to see another person as they really are, as emotional considerations are likely to bias our judgment.

But Paul doesn't mean that we should be coldly objective in our relationships. Rather, he wants us to understand that "knowledge and depth of insight" are the only means by which we can see another person clearly, fairly, and fully. The truth is that *we cannot be objective about another person unless we love them.*

Love is what enables us to see others' weaknesses with due consideration for their own struggles and the obstacles they have faced; to appreciate and accept others' uniqueness without judging based on our own preferences; to understand how they have been shaped by their upbringing and life experiences; and then to assess them fairly and generously.

Sometimes, what we call love has nothing to do with the other person. The loved one is simply an object upon whom we project our own needs, desires, and imagined attributes. But mature love accepts the other's personhood. In other words, we see him or her as a person who, like us, has needs, goals, desires, and joys, and we acknowledge that their interests are as important as our own. In fact, later in the letter to the Philippians, Paul reminds us that this is exactly how we are to think of others: "Each of you should look not only to your own interests, but also to the interests of others" (Phil. 2:4). In his letter to the church in Rome, Paul instructs them to "accept one another, then, just as Christ accepted you" (Rom. 15:7). In other words, accept others with full knowledge of who each person is and love them unconditionally.

While I see and affirm the beautiful vision of love and acceptance that Paul has presented to us, I have struggled to live accordingly. I've come to see that there is a black place in my own heart, one that finds expression in anger rather than love.

I've learned over time that I have a low frustration threshold. For one thing, I'm a perfectionist. Small flaws or discrepancies can annoy me far out of proportion to their importance. In addition, I lack patience, and I'm generally in a hurry. I can treat a five-minute delay as if it's a crime against humanity. I'm quick to become angry, and I'm equally quick to vent my anger on whatever it is that has gotten in my way. If a gasoline pump fails to print a receipt or a vending machine swallows my change, I usually punch it. When I stumble over something, I pause to kick it.

I can't honestly say that I have experienced any remorse over punching or kicking inanimate objects, except maybe the time I broke the windshield of my car by slamming my fist on it. I can't remember what I was angry about that day. I was certainly remorseful when I had to write the check to replace that windshield.

Then one day, a chance encounter helped me see that I sometimes treat people this same way—as if they were objects rather than fellow human beings. That day I was standing in line at an airport newsstand, waiting to pay for my purchase. The young woman serving the man ahead of me struggled with his transaction; she may have been a trainee. The man was frustrated with the delay and spoke cruel and demeaning words to the young cashier. His words flustered her; if she'd had any hope of solving the problem, it disappeared at that point. I could see that she was humiliated and was too upset to concentrate on what he wanted, which of course made an angry man even angrier.

Watching that young girl standing behind the register, it struck me that she was about the same age as my daughter, Park. And I remember thinking that, though she wasn't my daughter, this young woman was *someone's* daughter. Seeing her as someone's daughter, I felt a connection with her. She was not just the means of a transaction—she was a human being, with all the qualities that Park possesses.

The man's verbal abuse continued, and my indignation increased. Suddenly I realized, "This is what I look like sometimes." By failing to make this self-observation before that day, I had more than once allowed myself to be the customer from hell. Realizing that I had treated someone's daughter or son that way was painful to acknowledge, but it created a powerful motivation to change. I still struggle with the bad habit of giving rein to my anger, but I can honestly say that recognizing myself in this angry customer has produced lasting change in me.

The philosopher Jean-Luc Marion talks of "accepting the other's counter-gaze" as pivotal in defining our relationship with another person. When I acknowledge and accept another person's freedom to look into my eyes just as I look into theirs, I acknowledge that they are my equal.[17] In contrast, when I treat another person as if they are nothing more than a transaction machine, like an ATM, an automated gas pump, or a vending machine, I am not seeing them as fully human, and I am certainly not treating them as an equal.

One could argue that all injustice stems from this very notion: that the other person is somehow inferior to us, and therefore we are justified in treating him or her as less deserving. We need to acknowledge where the implications of this mindset can take us. Consider such large-scale acts of inhumanity as the Holocaust or America's experience with slavery.

Horrific injustice was condoned when many people rationalized that the Jewish people being persecuted or the black people who were enslaved were less than fully human.

Describing our transactional encounters with retail staff and service people in this way may seem extreme. Of course, committing genocide is a long, long step from treating a supermarket cashier rudely. Some of our passing interactions with other people in our daily lives may seem insignificant. And yet—can we truly gauge the impact of our actions on the lives of other people?

An incident a few years ago depicted for me the way in which an insignificant action can have a powerful impact. My wife and I were attending an evening function for a nonprofit organization. As we were walking from our car to the event venue, a woman who walked alongside of us glanced at me a couple of times, then introduced herself. She had recognized me from a newspaper photograph.

Several years earlier, she had interviewed me over the phone to do an article on my company. After the article appeared, I called her to compliment her on her work. By that point in my life, I had been interviewed by journalists several times, only to be annoyed by inaccuracies when I read the published article. Her article, though, was accurate and insightful, and I shared with her my high opinion of what she'd written.

For me, that quick phone call was simply the response of the moment, and one I soon forgot. But as we talked while walking to the event, she shared that the timing of my call had been powerful for her. She had just moved to our city with the goal of establishing herself as a freelance journalist. This article on my company was her first project. My phone call affirmed to her that she could excel at this work, and that her goal was achievable. In the years that followed that phone call, she had gone on to build a successful career.

I did a very small thing in calling her, yet its impact was lasting.

This incident was a fresh reminder for me to treat each interaction with other people as if it might change the course of their life—or mine. While I repeatedly fall short of this standard, striving for it has made a real difference in my behavior and interactions. It has been an effective practice, because it is rooted in the truth that each of us has dreams and goals, and we also have needs and insecurities. Each of us is hardwired to respond to kindness and encouragement. And each of us has moments when we need to have someone tell us the truth. You never know when the words you speak might be remembered for a lifetime.

Many of my important memories stem from incidents that were seemingly insignificant in and of themselves, yet I remember them because they evoked a powerful response from me.

One morning, early in my career, I came to my boss's office for a scheduled meeting. From behind his closed door, I could hear a notoriously hot-headed senior executive shouting at him. I was there to tell my boss something that I knew he wouldn't want to hear, so my tension mounted as the argument behind closed doors continued.

After the other executive stormed off, I walked into my boss's office. I expected him to explode when he heard my report, but he was patient and gracious with me. I could tell he was upset, but he dealt with me just as he would have at any other time.

He taught me a powerful lesson that day about the self-control that consideration for others requires from a leader. It was a defining moment for me, as both a person and a future business leader. I would guess, though, that my boss would not remember that occasion. It certainly wasn't a big event with lasting consequences; it was merely one of hundreds of meetings he and I had together during the three years I worked for him. That meeting's importance took place in my own head, and though his calmness and courtesy weren't unusual behavior for him, for me they powerfully reinforced the way his ethos shaped his responses to the daily situations he faced.

I remember reading an interview with Michael Jordan years ago, while he was still playing basketball with the Chicago Bulls. Jordan was noted for playing with intensity every single game during the long, grueling NBA season, whereas other, lesser players occasionally took a night off. The interviewer asked Jordan how he maintained his motivation. Jordan replied, and I paraphrase, "Every night there is someone in the stands who has never seen me play before. Their view of me as a basketball player will be formed forever by what they see that night." This thought gave Jordan the motivation to play his very best every game.

We are often unaware that we are creating defining moments for others. This truth highlights the importance of acting consistently, in things both small and large. *Living a life of love requires that we discipline ourselves to act lovingly always.*

In the same passage in Ephesians where Paul told us to "live a life of love," he also said, "Be kind and compassionate to one another, forgiving each other, just as in Christ God forgave you" (Eph. 4:32). You can never know the potential power of a word spoken in season. Conversely, you never know when a minor inconsistency could wreck a relationship. Our actions have the potential to *contradict* the values we profess as well as *reinforce* those values. In fact, such negative moments are even more likely to be remembered than positive moments. If you profess to value integrity, the one time you lie will be remembered far longer than the many times you told the truth. The lie is likely to be seen, not as an exception to who you are or your character, but as the time you let the mask fall to reveal your true self. We've all seen people who take credit for lofty values but don't make the effort required to live by them. This is much worse than professing no values at all.

Remember, one of the words you will speak today, or one of the decisions you will make, or one of the actions you will perform could have an impact that reverberates for years to come in the life of a co-worker, friend, family member, or even a chance acquaintance. This impact may magnify your effectiveness, or it may limit it profoundly. It could help shape the course of a young man or woman who looks up to you and watches everything you do.

If we could anticipate which word or action would be significant to others, we could always be prepared, but we can't know this ahead of time. Therefore, it's what you do spontaneously, in the moment, that reveals the person you are and has the potential to create a defining moment.

Embracing this knowledge enables us to love, whether that means celebrating another's success or graciously accepting their failure. And as our own love grows in knowledge and depth of insight, we are better able to translate the good we are motivated to do into actions that make the most of the opportunities we face.

I've come to believe that the network of our relationships comprises that which is the substance in our experience. How we live within these relationships determines the response that our lives evoke. When we think about the people we serve and the people who serve us—along with our families, neighbors, co-workers, and network of friends—the way that we handle these relationships is likely to prove more important than the work that they ostensibly support. Furthermore, our relationships are primarily composed of many small details, whose power is determined by whether they work together consistently toward loving, healthy ends. If you and I are remembered after we have left this earth, it will most likely be for our impact on people rather than for the outcomes of our projects. And so, Peter's list of qualities culminates with brotherly kindness and love. If my life does not embody love, no matter how great my faith or how glittering my gifts may be, "I am only a resounding gong or a clanging cymbal . . . I am nothing . . . I gain nothing" (1 Cor. 13:1–3).

And for this very reason, *who we are* is likely to loom far larger and have a greater impact than *what we do*. This brings us right back to where we started: "If you possess these qualities in increasing measure, they will keep you from being ineffective and unproductive in your knowledge of our Lord Jesus Christ" (2 Pet. 1:8).

If Peter's teaching is true, it should shape how we live. How, then, do we become the people God created us to be? How can we develop the qualities of character that will enable us to live a life of love? Let's turn now to exploring some practices that will help us grow.

part two

Engaging in Spiritual Disciplines

chapter ten

Introduction:
We Are Shaped by
What We Seek

a grand old oak tree stands in the backyard of a home where I lived for many years. Other trees cluster around it, some of them perhaps older than this oak. To gain access to the sun, this tree had to reach horizontally, growing fanwise, rather than vertically. All trees, to some extent, reveal the impact of their environment. A tree that grows without adaptation to its environment exists only in virtual worlds.

Humans also grow in response to their environment. When one path is blocked, we adapt, growing in a different direction to obtain what we need, or what we aspire to. We are much more than the sum of our external influences, but, like the oak tree I described, we are shaped in part by what we seek.

This begs the question: what should we seek?

It's wise to begin with the end in mind—a picture of the person we wish to become—so we can sow into our lives to produce the desired harvest. Paul expressed this principle very simply: "A man reaps what he sows" (Gal. 6:7). He goes on to encourage and assure us, "Let us not become weary in doing good, for at the proper time we will reap a harvest if we do not give up" (Gal. 6:9).

The implications of Paul's statement are profound: *each life that is lived faithfully has an impact for eternity.*

This is why Paul exhorted the church in Corinth, "Therefore, my dear brothers, stand firm. Let nothing move you. Always give yourselves fully to the work of the Lord, because you know that your labor in the Lord is not in vain" (1 Cor. 15:58). We can have an impact on the eternal destiny of the people we serve; the fruit of our work on their behalf will endure. When we live faithfully, intently, intelligently, and responsively to the leading of God's Spirit, "making the most of every opportunity" (Eph. 5:16), we offer a gift to God with which he is well pleased, and we also find the pathway for precious gifts that God wants to give us.

As Jesus finished the extended teaching that we know as the Sermon on the Mount, he said, "Everyone who hears these words of mine *and puts them into practice* is like a wise man who built his house on the rock" (Matt. 7:24, emphasis added).

Biblical teaching reinforces this point again and again. Hearing Jesus' words is not enough; we must put them into practice. The quote from Matthew 7 introduces the parable about the wise man who built his house on the rock. When the storms came, the house stood firm.

Pursuing growth in godly character is an essential element in building a house that stands. Character is not the rock on which we build; the rock and foundation is Christ. Paul teaches that "in the gospel a righteousness from God is revealed, a righteousness that is by faith from first to last" (Rom. 1:17). Likewise, developing godly character is first a step of faith. Building a resilient structure on that foundation defines the project of character development. Character comes not from what we can do to strengthen ourselves but from taking hold of the grace of God. As we train ourselves to do this, we develop the capacity to endure the inevitable storms that life brings, while fulfilling our potential to produce the fruit of a life well-lived.

In the chapters to come, we will explore spiritual and practical disciplines that can increase our capacity to live well, but an attitude of heart must underlie them all if God's goodness is to be infused into our lives. We are to seek after him with all our heart. If we seek him earnestly, we will find him. The Bible contains many promises; none have more powerful implications than the promise that we will find God if we seek him. Here are just a few of the verses that urge us to seek God, with the promise that he will respond:

- Those who seek the Lord lack no good thing (Ps. 34:10).
- O God, you are my God, earnestly I seek you; my soul thirsts for you, my body longs for you, in a dry and weary land where these is no water (Ps. 63:1).
- Blessed are they who keep his statutes and seek him with all their heart (Ps. 119:2).
- I love those who love me, and those who seek me find me (Prov. 8:17).
- You will seek me and find me when you seek me with all your heart (Jer. 29:13).
- He rewards those who earnestly seek him (Heb. 11:6).

The purpose of the spiritual disciplines is precisely this: to provide channels through which we can seek God. God can speak to us in many ways—through the words of our brothers and sisters in Christ, through Scripture, through preaching and teaching, through the prompting of the Holy Spirit as we pray, or as we go through our days.

Spiritual disciplines enable us to dig deep, ensuring that our character is founded on the Rock—the God who is. Practicing spiritual disciplines brings us into God's presence, enabling us to know him experientially. We learn the truth about God revealed to us in the Bible. And we learn to love the God we cannot see as we learn to love our sisters and brothers in the church—whom we can see and with whom we worship, serve, and learn.

What follows is not a comprehensive list of disciplines. The discussion here centers on the three disciplines that I consider foundational to every Christian's growth in maturity, and which I can write about from personal experience. For example, I have never actively practiced fasting; anything I write about it would be second-hand information from the experience of others.

We will begin with the practice of prayer. To build a foundation for powerful living, which can happen only as we are filled with God's power, we must learn to pray.

All of us have at least a working definition of prayer in our minds, but those definitions vary widely. What many Christians know of prayer is heavily influenced by their experience in church and other religious gatherings. The churches I've attended for most of my life practice spontaneous, unstructured public prayers. Sometimes these public prayers sound more like speeches to me, expressed in language that is unnaturally formal or studded with religious jargon. This isn't communication in any normal sense of the word.

Certainly there is power in voicing the shared values and beliefs within a community. Liturgical churches use prayers written for every occasion; some of those prayers have been used for centuries. There is comfort and assurance that comes from participating in well-remembered prayers shared by one's community. Sometimes, particularly in times of uncertainty or threat, public prayer expresses a shared yearning with powerful resonance. But while it is important for these reasons, public prayer alone is not sufficient for us. If we want a rich and intimate relationship with God, we need to practice personal prayer.

Accordingly, we need to practice solitude. If there is one spiritual discipline that is foundational for all the others, it is this one. This is true, in part, because spiritual solitude is uniquely foreign to the ultra-connected culture we live in. The length of time the solitude lasts is less important than the ability to be solitary during that time. This doesn't require outward solitude but rather an inward solitude. The question is not whether I am alone in a room, but whether I am concentrating completely on communicating with God. We will explore the practice of solitude in Chapter 11.

Next, we must learn to practice Paul's admonition to "pray continually" (1 Thess. 5:17), or, as the King James Version renders it, "pray without ceasing." When we return from solitude and reenter our world, we must learn how to remain in God's presence. This is the focus of Chapter 12.

In Chapter 13, we will discuss the discipline of reading and studying the Bible. What we can know of God is limited to what he chooses to reveal to us. The Bible is the primary source of God's revelation, and we are wise if we consistently explore its breadth and depth.

Prayer and Bible reading are primarily solitary activities; healthy spiritual growth also has a communal element. We need other voices to help us interpret accurately what God is teaching us through prayer and the Scripture. We need the experience of corporate worship as well as private worship. And we need to give and receive the loving support of brothers and sisters in Christ as we navigate a world that is hostile to God. Chapter 14 centers on the role that participation in a community of believers should play in our lives.

Let's explore these disciplines together.

chapter eleven

Practicing Solitude

*I*n his classic *The Spirit of the Disciplines*, the late Dallas Willard argued that solitude deserves "primacy and priority among the disciplines."[18] Here is his reasoning:

> The normal course of day-to-day human interactions locks us into patterns of feeling, thought, and action that are geared to a world set against God. Nothing but solitude can allow the development of freedom from the ingrained behaviors that hinder our integration into God's order.[19]

To have an adequate perspective on something we see, we often need to stand at a distance from it. The expression "can't see the forest for the trees" is hackneyed, but it creates a good picture of what I mean. We can be so close to something that we can no longer discern its true dimensions. We lack perspective on what is important and what is not.

But perceptual distance is not all we need. We live in a more intrusive culture than previous generations experienced. If you have a smartphone, you have immediate access to a range of information that no university library can match. You are barraged with breaking news and real-time information. You are also always within reach of everyone who knows you. And it's not only our personal electronic devices that break the silence. If you live in a community of any size, simply walk outside some evening, and listen. You'll soon realize that it's never actually quiet. Rural areas have their own soundtrack, though populated more by animals than machines.

Even indoors, in what we think of as the quiet of our homes, it's rarely quiet. If you listen, you are likely to hear climate control systems, appliances, and other devices whirring in the background. Noise incessantly accompanies the minutes and hours of our lives.

Because these sounds are always there, we rarely notice them. Accustomed to their presence, we go through our days without being aware of the stimuli in which we are immersed every waking hour.

Most of these sounds emanate from things that are good and useful. And yet it's also true that they all emanate from "a world set against God."

As I mentioned earlier, J. B. Phillips translates Romans 12:2 as: "Don't let the world squeeze you into its mould."[20] We are not always aware of the unremitting squeeze of our world's embrace. Unless we discipline ourselves to withdraw into solitude, we cannot maintain the distance to see the world and its pressures for what they are, nor can we have an accurate perspective on the God who is greater than all of it.

For many years, I have begun each new day with what many call a "quiet time." I have generally been the first to rise in my household, so mornings are a good time for me to seek solitude. During this time, I do my best to close out the world for forty minutes or more, while I read my Bible and pray.

Describing my devotional time in this way may make it sound more formulaic than it truly is. Time doesn't always fall neatly into two segments in which I first read from the Bible and then pray. As I read, I seek to concentrate on the "living and active" Word (Heb. 4:12, NRSV), with the confidence that God will speak to me through what I read. So I am interacting with the text, not simply reading it.

As many times as I have read through the Bible, I can still read well-remembered passages and be challenged by aspects of their meaning that I haven't fully grasped before. Sometimes, a recent experience enables me to read words in a new light.

When that happens, I may remember the way another translation treats a verse or phrase, then do an impromptu study to look more closely at what is being said. I may simply stop reading to ponder the passage I've just read.

At other times as I read, I am struck by some aspect of God's greatness or his goodness to me, and I put down my Bible and worship.

Often, what I read reminds me of someone, maybe a friend or family member who's facing a challenge or a need, and then I'll pray for them with words from the Scripture passage that speaks to their situation.

In the books I've read on spiritual disciplines, these practices are often described as discrete activities—study, meditation, worship, praise, thanksgiving, intercession. They can all be practiced in that way, and I sometimes do exactly that. However, in my experience, Bible reading, prayer, meditation, and intercession are often blended in my time of solitude. After all, if the Bible is God's Word, then it is his communication to us. Accordingly, when I am reading, I try always to be prepared for the possibility that he will use his Word to communicate specifically to me. There are many times when the passage of Scripture I happen to read on a particular morning speaks directly to an issue that I have been wrestling with. Other times, a verse puts me in mind of a friend or family member for whom I've been praying; when I share that verse with them in a letter, text, or phone call, God uses it to encourage them powerfully.

To share one example out of many, recently I was working through contentious and protracted negotiations with someone who had been a long-time colleague, and whom I considered a friend. The issues involved were complex, but I felt that my friend was experiencing personal pressures that kept him from negotiating in a fair-minded way. One Saturday morning, during a time when tensions were at their peak, my daily Bible reading brought me to the Sermon on the Mount. As I read the Beatitudes, I came to "blessed are the peacemakers" (Matt. 5:9), and the verse seemed to shout for my attention. I stopped, reflected, and prayed for a long time. It became apparent to me that God was speaking to me through this verse, and I realized that I needed to act as peacemaker with my old friend. The implications were potentially significant, because a great deal was at stake for me. I didn't interpret this to mean that I should simply say yes to every demand and allow myself to be abused by the process. However, I concluded that I needed to be willing to put my rights aside and do everything I could so that my friend could walk away from the negotiation contentedly. Furthermore, there were other people affected by this process, and I realized that making peace between the two of us would also be important to them, and for years to come.

There was sacrifice involved; I made financial and other concessions that my friend was not entitled to receive. But God spoke to me about this point also; as I was praying one morning a few weeks later, I reflected that my financial wellbeing comes from him alone. He was able to restore anything I needed. I concluded that God wanted me to obey his voice, spoken through that verse in my quiet time that morning, and trust him to provide for my needs.

In retrospect, I see that I have been blessed by choosing to be a peacemaker, just as Jesus promised. What I gave up is trivial in comparison with what I've received.

As you can see, as I pray each morning, I do so meditatively. When praying for a personal need or a challenge I'm facing, I don't simply ask for what I want. I try to step back as I view the situation, asking whether what I want is rooted in love or in selfishness, and whether it's best for the others who may be affected by the outcome. When I pray for someone, I don't merely read from a list of needs; I think about the person and ponder his situation. I may thank God for the good gifts that I'm aware of and ask that he work in my friend's life in his wisdom.

Thinking about friends, family members, and co-workers in this way often brings to mind some way in which I can be useful. As a result, sometimes the answers to prayer that I receive are the outcome of an action that I am prompted to take. Over the years, I've come to see how much of prayer's value comes not from God intervening in a situation but from God changing me and my perspective and then prompting me to act in response.

I've found that it takes consistent practice to have quiet time that achieves this purpose. Distracting thoughts are always vying for my attention, and they have many sources. I have a busy professional life, a family I love, several ministry involvements, and other relationships that are important to me. In the morning, my day's activities, requirements, and necessities are much on my mind. It's not easy to mentally detach myself from all these things and focus my attention completely on God. And yet I know that *if I don't treat solitude as an important priority and devote consistent time to it day after day, I will not succeed in placing enough distance between myself and the world to focus on God.* I don't know how someone can build a solid foundation for personal character unless this practice consistently nourishes their life. After all, character is formed not through what we can do to strengthen ourselves but from developing our ability to take hold of the grace of God.

Psalm 1, speaking of a godly man, says, "He is like a tree planted by streams of water, which yields its fruit in season and whose leaf does not wither. Whatever he does prospers" (Ps. 1:3). Solitude nourishes our spiritual roots. If the roots are not healthy, the tree is living on borrowed time. One day, a storm will reveal the tree's weakness and send it crashing to the ground.

The solitude I speak of can seem like anti-social behavior. It may at times require firmness with others to maintain it. If you're an extrovert, it may require ruthlessness with yourself. If solitude feels incompatible with your personality, you may even find it incomprehensible that being alone can possibly be good. You may conclude that this practice is one of those nice-but-not-essential things done by other people who are wired differently. But Richard Foster, reflecting on Jesus' habit of seeking solitude, draws a different conclusion: "Like Jesus, we must go away from people so that we can be truly present when we are with people."[21] These words, often attributed to the martyred missionary, Jim Elliot, provide sound advice: "Wherever you are, be all there." *The practice of solitude*, then, by enabling us to train ourselves to screen out distractions and to focus, not only roots us in a spiritually nourishing relationship with God but also *opens us up for deeper connection with other people.*

Finally, solitude establishes a place for us separate from the world and its pressures—not to mention the pressures we create for ourselves in response to the world, those John calls "the cravings of sinful man, the lust of his eyes and the boasting of what he has and does" (1 John 2:16).

Solitude opens a vantage point within our consciousness from which we can see the world's prizes, dreams, hopes, and obsessions for what they are. To keep the world from squeezing us into its mold, we must stand outside of the world's embrace. Sometimes, we must even stand outside the embrace of others. Solitude creates the space for us to do that.

It also offers a way, by faith, for us to build our priorities into our schedules. You may have read my earlier description of my daily quiet times and thought, "I could never set aside forty minutes a day for a quiet time." That may be true for you now; different seasons of life make different demands on us. For example, I have fewer demands on my time now that my children are grown than when my wife and I had young children in the house. And yet I maintained my daily quiet time throughout those child-rearing years. For me, it's not a matter of how busy I am but of what my priorities are.

I see setting aside time for solitude as similar to the practice of tithing to the church. If you start by reviewing your needs and try to determine whether you have anything left over to give to God, you will probably discover that you have little or nothing to give. However, if your starting point is to give generously and make your spending and saving decisions based on what you have left, then you will find that you can make the numbers fit. Setting aside time for solitude is not merely a discipline but a question of faith. Do I believe that if I begin my day with God, regardless of other things competing for my time, he is able to provide me with all the time I need to take care of my responsibilities? Do I believe that the universe can operate without my help for a few minutes each day? My answer to both questions, reinforced by many years of experience, is yes.

To persist in this practice until it becomes a habit, let me repeat my advice to take small steps. Don't start by trying to set aside forty minutes; start with just five or ten. The key is to form a daily discipline. After a while, your quiet time will become a habit that fits naturally within every day. If you can, anchor it to something that is already part of your routine. I start my days by making coffee. When it's ready, I pour a mugful, get my Bible, and find a quiet place.

Don't worry about how you will spend the time as you begin. First, stop. Orient your awareness on God's presence. If there is something you are hungry for, pursue it—knowledge, for example, from reading Scripture, or the chance to share your fears, doubts, concerns, questions. Remind yourself that it is rare to begin a relationship with an extended conversation. Long conversations come naturally when you know someone well, trust them, and share many interests. But a rich relationship must begin somewhere.

Let me caution you about the expectations you set for your experience of God's presence when you practice solitude. Practicing God's presence in solitude begins with believing that he is always present and then acting upon that belief. That doesn't mean that he will always manifest his presence to you. God is not a genie who can be summoned by rubbing a lamp.

This point may seem obvious, but I believe it goes deeper than we often realize. Earlier in this chapter I quoted the closing words of Hebrews 11:6; the verse begins with these words: "Without faith it is impossible to please God, because anyone who comes to him must believe that he exists." Doesn't that also seem obvious? But it seems to me that, for many believers, God is a concept, not a person. Practicing God's presence requires that we "believe that he exists"—that God is in fact a person, and that his existence is as real as that of the person beside me. In fact, God is beside me, now and always. In solitude, as we approach God, believing that he exists, we simultaneously draw closer to him and distance ourselves from the world. When we do this, we can live more freely.

chapter twelve

Praying Without Ceasing

For many years, I struggled to carry the peace and perspective that I had gained in my daily minutes of quiet and solitude into the workplace and the world. It was as though, after practicing deep breathing exercises, I took a final breath and gulped as much air into my lungs as I could, then ventured out while trying to hold my breath all day. None of us can hold our breath for very long.

I came to realize that, rather than expecting my quiet time to provide a daily spiritual oasis amid the desert, I had to learn how to irrigate the rest of my life. Only then could I go through my days feeling spiritually refreshed rather than spiritually worn down. God's provision for what I needed came through the practice of praying without ceasing.

I have a theory regarding biblical commands: if God commands us to do something, it is possible for us obey. Said another way, God won't command us to do something that can't be done. Furthermore, God's instruction is always for our good. If, as both Peter and Paul taught, the Scriptures were written for our instruction, these two points are hard to argue against. To command something impossible would be confusing and unhelpful. To command something harmful would be inconsistent with God's love for us.

While few may argue with this theory, in practice many of us treat God's commands as unrealistic. We may vaguely aspire to the standards that the Bible sets forth, but we don't act as though compliance is required.

Some of the Bible's commands are daunting. To take just a few examples:

- "Bless those who persecute you" (Rom. 12:14)
- "Do not worry about your life" (Matt. 6:25)
- "Love your neighbor as yourself" (Lev. 19:18)

Yet if they are possible to achieve—and, furthermore, if they are commanded—we need to re-examine our assumptions. And if we believe that all of God's commands are meant for our good, we should *want* to re-examine those assumptions.

When I started to follow God as a younger man, I stumbled at some point across these words from 1 Thessalonians 5:17: "pray continually," or as the King James Version has it, "pray without ceasing." Given the model of prayer that I had grown up with—uttering words in a reverent posture while attempting to focus completely on God—this command couldn't be interpreted literally.

However, I realized that taking my faith seriously meant that I couldn't simply dismiss or ignore a direct command. If the command seemed impossible, my understanding of the command must be incorrect.

I needed to understand what praying without ceasing really meant.

For more than twenty-five years now, I have been exploring what Paul is teaching in this verse. Praying without ceasing is the hardest of disciplines for me, but I have found that the best barometer of my spiritual health is whether I am consistently practicing it.

As I have come to understand and practice it, praying without ceasing means that I am living in full awareness of God's presence and communicating with him as with a companion. I don't mean that I think of God as my buddy, on a par with me. And though God is immeasurably greater than I am, I don't think he wants me to relate to him as a superior who is always looking critically over my shoulder. Jesus told his disciples, "I no longer call you servants, because a servant does not know his master's business. Instead, I have called you friends" (John 15:15).

In his book *The Practice of the Presence of God*, Brother Lawrence expresses this premise very simply: "The presence of God is the concentration of the soul's attention on God, remembering that he is always present."[22] This enduring spiritual classic was written by a monk who worked as a kitchen helper. The humble nature of his work was no barrier to experiencing God's presence. God is just as present when we are washing dishes as when we are reading the Bible or sitting in church.

A recent visit with my son James and daughter-in-law Eunice in New York City crystallized this truth for me. I wanted to visit a couple of museums during my stay, so James set aside a day for us to spend together. We walked a great deal that day, and as we walked there were several stretches of time when we were both silent. Our silence didn't stem from an awkwardness but because we felt no need to talk (I should note that we are both men of few words). Throughout that day, I was always conscious of my son's presence with me in a way that was filled with joy and gladness. We communicated often, but spoken words were not always needed.

The Greek word translated "continually" in the NIV and "without ceasing" in the KJV is *adialeiptós*. It does not indicate non-stop praying but prayer that is constantly recurring. Devotional author Henri Nouwen put it this way:

> To pray unceasingly . . . would be completely impossible if it meant to think constantly about God. To pray, I think, does not mean to think about God in contrast to thinking about other things, or to spend time with God instead of spending time with other people. Rather, it means to think and live in the presence of God.[23]

Elsewhere, Nouwen describes prayer as "the basic receptive attitude out of which all of life can receive new vitality."[24] This is akin to my experience. It doesn't *exclude* speaking to God. Yet like that day in New York City walking with my son, while always mindful of his presence, speaking and listening is merely one part of the time that we spend with God.

Though I live in a world where God is always present, I am not always mindful of his presence. But when I go through my days with that awareness, it changes how I think, what I think about, and how I respond to circumstances and people and challenges.

When I am mindful of God's presence, I am quick to pray when I need wisdom or patience, or when I need to exhibit kindness or self-control. Paul refers to these traits and behaviors as the "fruit of the Spirit" (Gal. 5:22). Traversing my days with awareness of God's presence opens my heart so that his Spirit can produce this fruit.

Such mindfulness also helps me see that my days are opportunities for joy. My personality sometimes leads me to see my days as filled with heavy burdens to be lifted. As I process challenges and problems in my ongoing conversation with God, I am better able to see them as the opportunities they are. God has placed these things in my day for his good purpose. James tells us, "Consider it pure joy, my brothers, when you face trials of many kinds" (Jas. 1:2). That is not a crazy way to think; it is realistic and rational when we live in the confidence that God is present with us and is able to bring about what he desires in any and every circumstance. And we can take joy in the knowledge that the challenge facing us, along with the strength he gives us to meet it, are part of his redemptive plan. He doesn't need us to do any of this, but in his goodness, he invites us to participate in his work.

This perspective has practical meaning for me every day. Currently, I serve in an executive role with an industrial company, a leadership role in my church, consulting roles with several other businesses and ministries, and as a mentor for several younger leaders. I often find myself in discussions where my counsel is sought, and I am prompted to pray silently as those conversations begin and proceed. When someone comes to me for counsel or simply to share a difficulty they are facing, I recognize that my words may affect the course they will take. This is an important responsibility. Such an encounter is also an opportunity— *God* has brought this person into my life, and I want to fulfill the trust that he has reposed in me. If wisdom is sought, I ask God to enable me to speak words of wisdom and truth. Sometimes, as I'm listening to the other person, I'll ask God to help me understand accurately and comprehensively what is being said and help me to ask the right questions.

When I describe what I mean by praying without ceasing, it may sound easy, like adapting to a natural rhythm. But as I mentioned earlier, I have found it a difficult discipline. Other believers have told me that their experience is similar. I am not sure why it's difficult, but perhaps it is because there are many ways to get off track. For one thing, praying without ceasing reflects not only mutuality but dependence. I have always found it easy to revert to an assumption of self-sufficiency rather than dependence. I am also used to thinking that there is a clear-cut difference between processing life alone or processing life with others. In fact, I am never alone, and my thoughts are never private. This realization can be disconcerting, especially at those times when my spirit is angry or annoyed with someone and I want to indulge myself in hostile or complaining thoughts. However, if God is always present, sin is never okay.

Even so, I confess that sinfulness still holds many attractions for me, misleading though those attractions are. It can be a battle to move through my days with a prayerful, responsive spirit always mindful of God's presence and desirous to do his will. But this battle is one that I know I need to fight. While I face the need to allow God to change me so that I look more and more like his Son, this discipline is essential. When I think of what it means to surrender all that I am to God, this challenge frames both the struggle and the opportunity.

The struggle is to bring God into every area of my life, all the time. As I seek to do this, his displeasure with sinful habits of thought, whether lust or resentment or whatever it may be, becomes evident. In those moments, I can choose to turn toward obedience or turn away from it.

When I was younger, there was a sense in which I thought that, at some point in my life, all my sin would be dealt with. I wouldn't have stated it this way, yet this misconception was implicit in how I thought about my own distant future. Now, though, I see that dealing with one's sinfulness is more like peeling away layers of an onion. God enables me to recognize a sinful pattern of thinking or acting and then enables me to deal with it. Once it's removed, the next sinful pattern becomes apparent.

The issues have changed as I have grown in my faith. The sins I struggle against now tend to be more subtle—matters of motivation and intention rather than overt sinful action. When I was a boy, I sometimes punched my brother when he got on my nerves (which he often endeavored to do). I'm never tempted to punch my brother these days, but I have other temptations. I am convinced that I will never get to the end of rooting out sin in my life.

There are also opportunities that come from a posture of continual prayer, and I find them to be powerfully motivating. I appreciate the way J. B. Phillips translates Philippians 1:10: "I want you to be able always to recognize the highest and the best, and to live sincere and blameless lives until the day of Jesus Christ."[25] I've come to see that every challenge, every question, and every decision has the potential to fulfill "the highest and the best."

When I think about and pray about decisions affecting my children, friends, co-workers, and others, I often ask myself, "What is the highest and best outcome that is possible in this situation?" Sometimes, the immediate issue isn't the most important issue at stake. By reframing the context, I have made better decisions and taken more helpful actions. Sometimes the decision seems weighty, and other times it seems small. Over the years, though, I have learned that God's ability to work powerfully in and through a situation is not a function of its seeming importance.

When we think of fulfilling our potential, of living in a way that bears much fruit, we generally think of the *big* things. Have I found a vocation in which I can excel? Have I found a ministry where I can use my gifts consistently and powerfully? These are good questions, but we have the process backwards. In truth, we fulfill the potential of each moment by moving through our days with a spirit that is attentive to God and receptive to the promptings of his spirit. This posture needs to be our focus; when it is, we will find that the big decisions are wisely made.

Jesus said, "I am the vine; you are the branches. If a man remains in me and I in him, he will bear much fruit; apart from me you can do nothing" (John 15:5). Praying without ceasing is the method of abiding and leads to much fruit. Without it, no matter how impressive the external accomplishments, God sees them as "nothing."

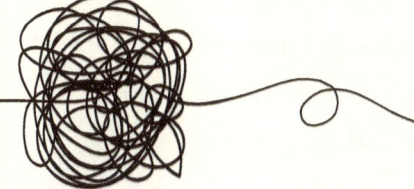

chapter thirteen

Studying the Scriptures

ible study and prayer go hand in hand. Jesus has opened the way for us to have a personal relationship with his Father. Prayer is our means of exploring that relationship, but we must ensure we are pursuing the God who is there, not a god whose contours are traced by our imagination or defined by our needs and wants. As we noted earlier, we can know no more of God than he reveals to us, and the Bible is our primary source of revelation.

As we explore what the Bible can teach us, consider the following passage from the book of Deuteronomy. Deuteronomy comprises Moses' farewell address to the people of Israel. They are about to enter the Promised Land after forty years in the wilderness. Moses will not be entering the land with them. He reviews what he and they have learned together and offers advice on how to meet the challenges that lie ahead. One day, Moses tells them, Israel will be led by a king. Here is what Moses said the king must do:

> When he takes the throne of his kingdom, he is to write for himself on a scroll a copy of this law. . . It is to be with him,

and he is to read it all the days of his life so that he may learn to revere the Lord his God and follow carefully all the words of this law and these decrees *and not consider himself better than his brothers.* (Deut. 17:18–20, emphasis added)

The king is to treat the Scriptures with the utmost seriousness and importance. He is to transcribe his own copy by hand and then read it every day. Both tasks will embed the teaching in his mind. The king is to "follow carefully *all* the words of this law" (emphasis added), so he must read it from beginning to end. And he is to do this so he can learn to first, revere God; second, follow God's commands; and third, "not consider himself better than his brothers."

If asked why we read the Bible, I suspect that most of us would answer with some combination of the first and second reasons. But reason three is no less central to the Bible's message. If we read the Bible and ponder its teachings, we understand that we are no better than anyone else, no matter how successful we may be in the things that matter most to us and our culture. And as we read, we are likely to realize that we sometimes repeat the mistakes made by one of the Bible's sinful characters (and all its human characters except Jesus are sinful to at least some degree). Or we may see that we are cherishing sinful thoughts or attitudes.

The writer of Hebrews tells us, "The word of God is living and active . . . it judges the thoughts and attitudes of the heart" (Heb. 4:12). When we read the Bible attentively, we can gain insight into ourselves, both who we are and who we have the potential to become, fueling a desire and creating the capacity to grow and change. Time with the Bible is an essential practice if we are to possess the qualities of Christian character in increasing measure.

The knowledge we gain from reading Scripture is good, but the biblical writers affirm again and again that knowledge without application is pointless. James writes:

"Do not merely listen to the word, and so deceive yourselves. Do what it says. Anyone who listens to the word but does not do what it says is like a man who looks at his face in a mirror and, after looking at himself, goes away and immediately forgets what he looks like. But the man who looks intently into the perfect law that gives freedom, and continues to do this, not forgetting what he has heard, but doing it—he will be blessed in what he does." (Jas. 1:22–25)

Let me caution you on this point, because *attempting to apply the Bible's teaching without understanding its breadth will create problems* of its own. If we base important decisions or life patterns on something we know inaccurately or incompletely, we are likely to make mistakes.

I suspect it has always been the case that many Christians have limited biblical knowledge. The proportion of serious readers in every generation is relatively small, and, in most eras, lack of access to the Bible offset the high reverence in which it was held. In contemporary America, even some pastors are unacquainted with large segments of biblical teaching. They are familiar with the best-known stories, and they may foray into less-well-trodden passages from time to time. However, they lack a sense for the breadth of biblical teaching, particularly on the more difficult and complex issues of doctrine or ethics. As Jesus said, "If a blind man leads a blind man, both will fall into a pit" (Matt. 15:14).

Even if your pastor *is* a great theologian, though, merely attending church and listening to a sermon once a week will not instill the biblical knowledge that each of us needs.

I have developed the habit each morning of spending time reading the Bible and praying. I have used devotional books at times but have found that reading the Bible itself rather than commentaries on the Bible is more consistently helpful and challenging. I have also spent time studying various teachings in depth, often in preparation for my own teaching, but also to learn more about issues I struggle with or hope to better understand.

When studying, I have learned to seek out books that will help me read the Bible with fresh eyes, including books written by theologians and other thinkers who reside at different points on the theological spectrum than I do. Looking at the Bible from different perspectives has helped me see that the lenses through which I view and interpret Scripture have been shaped by the teaching I have received and by my personal background more than I realized. Seeing how believers from different faith traditions, backgrounds, and eras approach and interpret the Scripture helps me to read what is actually there, not simply *see* what I have been taught to see or what I have always seen.

Over the years, I have read the Bible all the way through from Genesis to Revelation more than twenty times. I cannot overstate the importance of this practice in educating my mind and training my heart. As I strive to understand how to live right in a world full of wrongs—specifically, how to express love in word and action, not only as an individual but through the roles I play in institutions—having a solid sense of what is often called "the whole counsel of God" has been invaluable.

For example, have you ever observed that there are books of the Bible that seem to point in different directions? Some people argue that the Bible's teachings contain confusing contradictions. I see these seemingly contradictory teachings as presenting point and counterpoint on how to interpret the uncertainties that surround decisions we must make, and how to assess the trade-offs that life requires of us.

For example, the book of Proverbs contains many aphorisms that express the rewards that come to those who live wisely. In contrast, the fierce realist who wrote Ecclesiastes challenges us to consider that "the race is not to the swift or the battle to the strong, nor does food come to the wise or wealth to the brilliant or favor to the learned; but time and chance happen to them all" (Eccl. 9:11). But do Proverbs and Ecclesiastes really contradict one another? To this question, I would answer, only if you think there needs to be one right answer to all of life's questions.

This has not been my life experience in the fallen world we live in. Our knowledge, no matter how extensive or well informed, can only be incomplete and partial. There are conflicting truths whose depths we cannot plumb. *When faced with unanswerable questions, we may find that seemingly opposed perspectives each have something important to teach.* This is yet another way in which Scripture teaches us humility: by helping us to see the incompleteness and inadequacy of our knowledge and understanding. Paul admonished Timothy:

> The holy Scriptures . . . are able to make you wise for salvation through faith in Christ Jesus. All Scripture is God-breathed and is useful for teaching, rebuking, correcting and training in righteousness, so that the man of God may be thoroughly equipped for every good work. (2 Tim. 3:15-17)

It isn't that the Bible contains answers to every question—far from it. But I have come to see that the Bible presents the truth about life. It deals honestly with the complexity of people and with the complexity of the communities and cultures humans have created.

Yes, Christians have a wide range of views on how to interpret Scripture. The most hard-fought controversies often center on what I consider side issues, such as whether the creation account in Genesis 1 is meant to be interpreted literally or figuratively. I think we can acknowledge that these issues generally arise in good faith. But it raises the question: if as Paul teaches, "all Scripture is God-breathed," what does that mean for us as we seek to interpret and understand the Bible?

Most people tend to adopt the interpretive assumptions held by the faith tradition in which they were raised. Or if we come to faith as adults, we are likely to adopt the teaching we receive at the beginning of our faith journey. But there are sincere believers in different traditions, also seeking to discern the truth in good faith.

Like many students of the Bible, I have formed conclusions about many of these issues. However, my point is not to come down on one side or another. I think much dispute could be avoided if we limited ourselves to affirming what Scripture affirms about its own purpose—"to make you wise for salvation . . . equipped for every good work" (2 Tim. 3:15, 17). This is the role that study of Scripture plays as we earnestly seek after God.

chapter fourteen

Practicing Community

The spiritual disciplines we have explored thus far are practiced in solitude. As we've seen, solitude provides a powerful and, I believe, necessary resource for seeking after God. However, to experience a flourishing spiritual life, we need to balance our times of solitude with life in community with other believers. Solitude that is not balanced by healthy relationships can lead to self-absorption. As we participate in a fellowship of believers, worshipping together and supporting each other, we are reminded that we as individuals are not the center of God's universe, and that we were not designed to stand alone.

In one sense, participating in a church, particularly in the practice of corporate worship, brings benefits that parallel the ones we receive from practicing solitude. Like solitude, worshipping among other believers pulls us away from the smothering embrace of the prevailing culture, immersing us in an environment suffused with a different source of meaning. Worship services provide space for people to encounter God outside the distractions and pressures of the world we live in.

The COVID-19 shutdowns in 2020 created a months-long hiatus between in-person worship services for most churches. When services resumed, people were slow to return to church. Even years later, many churches have never fully recovered their attendance. At our church, the proportion of people who attend online is much higher than it was before the pandemic.

It's interesting to me that the practice of disengaging from the church was already a concern in the first century, when the church began. The writer of Hebrews urges us to not give up meeting with other believers as some were in the habit of doing, but to meet together to spur one another on in love and good deeds (Heb. 10:24–25).

It takes time and effort to attend worship services. It can be hard to find a congregation where people, theology, and approach to worship are compatible with our preferences. And yet the Bible teaches us that this effort is worthwhile and is, in fact, necessary for spiritual health. There is an indefinable power among believers when they come together. We may not understand it, but the power is there. Jesus promised, "Where two or three come together in my name, there am I with them" (Matt. 18:20). Public worship is also a way to affirm that we belong to Christ.

The multitude of church congregations around the world reflects very different approaches to worship and community life. For many years, I have belonged to a large, nondenominational evangelical church that focuses on reaching unchurched people in our community. Accordingly, our music and the communications media we use are adapted from cultural models. I have good friends who attend some of the excellent Anglican churches in our community, where the worship services are rooted in a time-honored liturgy. The services at our church may be an easier step for an unchurched person to take, but the nature of a contemporary service means that the historic roots of the faith can be harder to discern.

In contrast, at an Anglican service, I am reminded that I am not just part of a church today, but part of a chain that links the past to its future. Neither approach is the right or wrong way to approach God, nor are the many styles of worship in between the two. The wide variation among congregations and worship styles reflects the differences between people—their background, their makeup, and their needs. Peter teaches that "you also, like living stones, are being built into a spiritual house to be a holy priesthood, offering spiritual sacrifices acceptable to God through Jesus Christ" (1 Pet. 2:5). All the varied congregations of Christ-followers around the world are spiritual stones comprising a larger edifice that God is building through Christ for his glory.

It is customary for worship services to include a time of teaching, and this too is valuable. Each of us needs to develop a personal familiarity with Scripture, as we've seen, but we also need a sound theological framework within which to ground our learning. By participating in a church with well-thought-through and well-articulated beliefs, we are better able to avoid error in our own beliefs.

The church's teaching is part of God's provision for his children. Paul's words in 1 Corinthians 12 explain that the teachers and pastors who equip us for the work of the ministry have received their spiritual gifts from God, to be exercised within the context of the church.

It is also important to recognize that "to each one the manifestation of the Spirit is given for the common good" (1 Cor. 12:7). In fact, all the spiritual gifts distributed by the Spirit, not just those given to teachers and pastors, are to be exercised within the church.

And so another reason we need the church is that *we need our brothers and sisters*. In addition to a framework for belief, a church, through its members, our brothers and sisters in Christ, provides support and encouragement, even rebuke when needed, when trials and difficulties can cause belief to falter. Proverbs 27:17 tells us, "As iron sharpens iron, so one man sharpens another."

The support we receive from our church takes many forms. I spent a number of years actively working with homeless people, and I came to see that the reason some fall into homelessness and others don't is not primarily because some stumble and others don't. All of us can stumble. It's because some people have a support network, family and friends who help them up when they stumble, whereas others lack that support.

When my wife Penny developed a rare form of leukemia and eventually endured a bone marrow transplant, the range and depth of support we received from our church was extraordinary. As a caregiver spending weeks in the transplant section of the cancer hospital, I came to see that patient survival was closely correlated to the amount of support the caregiver received. Everyone had a caregiver, but few survived if their caregiver had to go it alone, unsupported by others.

In my case, many caregivers came alongside me, enabling my wife to receive care far beyond what I could have given, and giving me opportunities for rest that enabled me to endure better than if I had been on my own. Others brought meals—one family brought us a meal each week for a year—while others cleaned our home. One woman took my growing early-teen daughter clothes shopping (while they were out, my daughter told her, "It's so embarrassing to go shopping with your dad."). Another couple provided a haven for our seventeen-year-old son; he spent a couple of evenings at their house every week.

Many people prayed for us. The impact of that prayer can be hard to discern; what did God do in response? What problems did he forestall that I never saw because they never happened? There is no definitive answer. I can tell you that I felt prayed for, and that knowledge alone was powerfully encouraging. I also noticed that everything outside of Penny's care went smoothly in those years. Out of the fifteen years that I led my company, those years saw fewer issues than any others. Another concern was my own health; Penny was immunosuppressed for years, and I wondered how I would care for her if I became sick. I didn't; for a couple of years, I never even caught a cold. I believe prayer had a role in that.

Very few of us will go through our lives without at least one period of grave need. Support is an essential role of the church.

A final reason we need the church is implied in what we have just reviewed: when we are part of a body that cares for all the other parts, we also have a responsibility. Paul tells us, "Now you are the body of Christ, and each one of you is part of it" (1 Cor. 12:27). Each of us has been given gifts for the common good. We need to join a community of believers, because just as we need our brothers and sisters, *our brothers and sisters need us* to exercise the gifts God has given us on their behalf.

Many churches teach that each of us has a special *gift*, and that gift is held out to us in the form of a "calling." We need to search until we find that gift. As we learn to exercise our gift, we discover our calling, and we are to walk out that calling from that time forward.

Our attempt to layer theology onto the simple question *What is my spiritual gift?* reflects our culture's preoccupation with self-fulfillment rather than biblical principles. If we seek first to fulfill ourselves through our service, we may find that we are serving only ourselves. I also question the way we usually talk about the role that one's "calling" plays in one's life.

Certainly, some people do receive a lifelong calling. Paul introduced himself to the Roman church in this way: "Paul, a servant of Christ Jesus, called to be an apostle and set apart for the gospel of God" (Rom. 1:1). The Greek word translated here as "called" denotes being set apart for a special purpose. God specifically chose Paul for the extraordinary role of an apostle; what we might term a calling with a capital C.

It may surprise you to learn that this Greek word is rarely used in the New Testament, and never in the Gospels.

In contrast, the Greek word usually translated "call" or "calling" has a much less elevated meaning. For example, Luke records that, while traveling through Asia (modern-day Turkey) during what we call the Second Missionary Journey, Paul had a vision in the night of a man from Macedonia "standing and begging him, 'Come over to Macedonia and help us.' After Paul had seen the vision, we got ready at once to leave for Macedonia, concluding that *God had called us to preach the gospel to them*" (Acts 16:9–10, emphasis added).

Luke uses this same word to describe what happened after Peter and John stood before the Jewish council, having been ordered not to preach in the name of Jesus (Acts 4:18). Rather than a special anointing for a special purpose, *calling* is a commonplace word that one would use to beckon someone. It does not imply that, once beckoned, a person is expected to remain in that place forever.

My point is this: don't try to "discover your calling" as if it's a *thing* that's out there to be found. Rather, think of your calling as a function of what you love to do, and how that love marks out a distinctive path of service within the church and in the world.

Frederick Buechner once defined vocation as "the place where your deep gladness meets the world's deep need."[26] It begins with understanding both the potentialities and the limitations with which God has shaped you, and then learning how to develop and deploy them so that you can be fruitful. As you do this, you will discover potentialities that you can develop for the rest of your life.

Our circumstances, whatever they might be, contain opportunities for us to serve God, and we should be continually alert for ways that he can use us. As Paul said elsewhere, "For we are God's workmanship, created in Christ Jesus to do good works, which God prepared in advance for us to do" (Eph. 2:10).

We are surrounded by people who need Christ, people with invisible wounds of all kinds, people who are hungry, people who are lonely and sad. If we are sensitive to the Spirit's prompting, we will be alert to these needs and seek to meet them. The form our actions take will vary depending on our talents, resources, and time, but we can trust God to empower us for the tasks he sets before us. *This is what spiritual gifts are—God's power at work through us to accomplish his will.*

Our culture's influence leads many to adopt a consumer mindset when it comes to church. We think primarily about what we are receiving; we assess its quality and may leave if we find a more attractive option or cease to feel that our church is effectively meeting our needs. Of course, there are legitimate reasons to change churches; we will review this question further in Chapter 18 on commitment. And as we've seen, the benefits we receive from a church are important to our spiritual flourishing, which is why the Bible teaches the importance of belonging to a local group of believers.

However, important as these benefits are, what we get must be paired with what we give. Active participation in a church requires a commitment to serve, as well as a willingness to be served. Learning to give, learning to receive, and learning to worship joyfully side by side are all part of why we're there.

In our culture, especially after COVID-19, there's nothing automatic about showing up regularly for Sunday worship and becoming actively involved in the life of your church. It's a commitment you make for yourself as well as for other members of the congregation. If you fail to make this commitment, you cheat yourself and others of the benefits of multiple God-given gifts. In Hebrews 10:25, when we hear the voice of Scripture saying, "Let us not give up meeting with other believers, as some are in the habit of doing," it's one of the times when we need to soften our hearts.

part three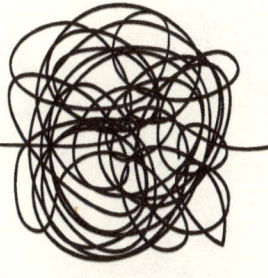

Developing
Productive Habits

chapter fifteen

Introduction: The Power of Habit

In the central scriptural passage for this book, Peter teaches that developing godly qualities of character will keep us from "being ineffective and unproductive in [our] knowledge of our Lord Jesus Christ" (2 Pet. 1:8). As we put biblical teachings into practice, we are forced to recognize patterns of thinking and acting that are inconsistent with godly living. Real change must result in acting differently.

The Bible teaches that our actions reveal who we are. Good trees produce good fruit, as Jesus taught: "By their fruit you will recognize them" (Matt. 7:16).

The need for godly thinking and acting is easy to understand but hard to do. Training ourselves to respond consistently to God's voice, consistently expressing love through constructive action, does not happen overnight; changing entrenched patterns of behavior takes time and effort. But actions that are consistently repeated have the power to shape us over time.

Do you see the implication of this line of thought? Yes, our character is expressed through action, as a good tree is revealed by its good fruit, but it is also true that our character is *developed* through action. The disciplines we adopt to implement change help to shape the people we become.

The word *discipline* puts me in mind of a profusely sweating athlete powering through a high-intensity workout. On the other hand, the word *habit* makes me think of flossing teeth. It is a modest little word— but then living well is a modest endeavor, for the most part. It doesn't require heroics, and that's good, because heroics cannot be sustained for long. Living a life of love isn't built on spurts of effort but on consistent behavior.

Disciplines are not ends in themselves; rather, they are the means of arriving at a healthy way of living. In other words, the purpose of disciplines, which we cannot sustain for long, is to build good habits that we can sustain. And so it is, that practicing wisely chosen habits is a more reliable path to loving relationships and impactful work than grand vision, audacious goals, or disciplined intensity.

A great little book—*The Power of Habit* by Charles Duhigg[27]—helped me understand this. It's an outstanding survey of current research on how habits are formed, sustained, and changed. There were many "aha" moments for me as I read, and I recommend the book highly. It proved helpful both in my personal life and in my leadership roles; the chapters on keystone habits for organizations are brilliant.

Duhigg makes the point that we cannot overcome a bad habit through sheer willpower. When we try this, we crave the reward that was embedded in the habit—and that reward is the reason we adopted the habit in the first place. The craving intensifies as hours and days go by; few people can resist its power all the way to changing the habit.

However, though we can't simply drop bad habits, we can replace them with good habits. By discerning the reward we receive from a habit we wish to change, we can consciously embed a replacement reward in a new set of actions. This doesn't eliminate the need for willpower, but it makes the habit-change process much easier, so our limited resources of willpower can accomplish it successfully.

Sometimes we take this step unconsciously. I have been very consistent in having a quiet time each morning for many years. I have gone for entire years without missing my quiet time for a single day, and when I do miss, it's usually because I'm traveling and not in control of my environment or my schedule. After reading Duhigg's book, I realized that a powerful reinforcement to this important habit is the spiritually unimportant habit of morning coffee. The first thing I do in the morning is make a pot of coffee; when my coffee is ready, I pour myself a mug, pick up my Bible, and begin my quiet time.

As any of you who are coffee drinkers will attest, I don't have to work at maintaining my morning coffee habit. Without me realizing it, tying my morning coffee to my quiet time made that habit easy to maintain as well.

Much of life consists of our habitual behaviors. Each of us has developed the ability to accomplish many tasks with minimal intervention from our conscious minds. Thinking consumes prodigious amounts of energy, and we can't sustain it for very long, just as we can't sprint for long distances. Our habits enable us to preserve our capacity to think for situations when thinking is really needed. They do this by freeing us from the need to make decisions about everything we do.

Why is it that we so often fall far short of our aspirations for godly living? It is because we think we can move easily from one way of living to another, and that is not possible. Habits change slowly. Furthermore, our capacity for changing our habits is limited. We are forced to work in our conscious minds when we adopt a new habit. Time and energy are needed for that new habit to become automatic. If we can change one habit at a time, we're doing well. But a habit, once changed, tends to stay in place. While the process of changing habits is slow, it is sure. We really can build upon this process.

If you want to grow, spiritually or otherwise, setting realistic goals is important, but it is only a first step, which must be coupled with two other things. First, nothing is likely to change in your life unless you carefully consider how you will take constructive steps forward. Second, no change is likely to last unless it is embedded in habits that are woven into the pattern of your daily life. You need to figure out:

- Where you want to go—beginning with the end in mind, take time to visualize what success will look like when your planned change has taken hold
- What to change in your daily or weekly or monthly patterns of living to arrive at your goal
- How you will set this change in motion
- And finally, how you will discipline yourself to practice this change until it becomes habitual

A structure, once built, stays in place in the same form, subject to the impact of time and the elements. A living person, though, renews their life day by day. Each day, we make decisions that determine whether we will continue on the path that leads to life or drift away from it. We also choose the pace at which we go.

If you've read this far, you have decided to choose the path of life.

Now, let's examine the life habits that can enable us to "run with perseverance the race marked out for us" (Heb. 12:1).

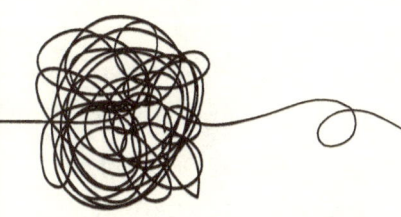

chapter sixteen

Cultivating a Responsive Heart

n an earlier chapter, we read this challenge from the book of James: "Who is wise and understanding among you? Let him show it by his good life, by deeds done in the humility that comes from wisdom" (Jas. 3:13). James is teaching us that *wisdom that grows from knowledge of the Scriptures expresses itself in a life well lived.*

How do we recognize "deeds done in the humility that comes from wisdom"? I believe that any act of service performed in love meets this test. But I have learned that genuine expressions of love sometimes require us to serve in ways that are humbling. Love will sometimes lead us to perform tasks that don't require special talent, that seem to have little impact, and that may be unrewarded. The "humility that comes from wisdom" doesn't require that we make a point of seeking out such acts of service, but it does require that we are open to taking them on.

This orientation stands in direct opposition to our culture's version of wisdom, where high achievers are taught to focus their time strategically. Every fragment of time and energy must be fully exploited and utilized as we strive to achieve high-value results. We are told to prioritize relationships with people who can advance our careers or impart something else of value, people who are important because of the power they wield or the wealth they possess. Similarly, we are trained to focus on high-value tasks, which we usually measure in terms of their scope or range of potential impact. We spiritualize this teaching by relating it to stewardship. Surely we want to do our best with the resources that God has entrusted to us. Isn't that what the parable of the talents teaches? However, living this way gives us a distorted view of life and of ourselves.

James has harsh words for those who treat wealthy, powerful people one way and other people differently: "If you show favoritism, you sin" (Jas. 2:9).

We know God doesn't value us based on our accomplishments or wealth. If everyone has equal dignity and value in his eyes, then we can't gauge the value of an act of service by the "importance" of the person we are serving, or by the number of people that may be impacted. God loves and values many people who wouldn't necessarily seem important to us. Indeed, if we see person X as important and person Y as unimportant, we are not seeing as God sees. If we are going to serve God rather than being misled by false values, then we need to be attentive and open to his guidance.

How do we ensure we are open to his guidance? The answer is likely to be different for each of us. For example, I am a planner. I schedule most of my days in meticulous detail so I can make the best use of my time. Several years ago, as I was meditating about the admonition in Hebrews, "Today, if you hear his voice, do not harden your hearts" (Heb. 3:15), the question occurred to me: How do I discern his voice amid all the competing voices that fill my days? What might it look like if God were trying to get my attention?

It struck me that his voice might well come to me in the form of an interruption. In my zeal for productivity, I usually respond poorly to interruptions. I tend to see them as obstacles to be brushed aside or overcome so I can stay on track with my goals for the day or week or month.

But what if God had a priority for me that my planning didn't envision? What if he were to bring someone into my life with a need I am equipped to meet—perhaps even uniquely equipped? Would I put aside my own priorities and respond to that person, or would I push them away? Would I view the interruption as an opportunity from God or as an obstacle to my agenda?

I quickly realized that I would be most likely to see only the interruption and miss the opportunity. This was a disturbing realization. I had always seen my tenacity and personal drive as good things, and now I saw that they could lead me to harden my heart to God's purpose for me in that moment.

One of my favorite biblical stories records an incident when Jesus was interrupted. It is recorded in Matthew, Mark, and Luke; we will look at Mark's version, which is the most detailed and vivid. If, as tradition has it, Mark is recording Peter's eyewitness account, this story must have had a powerful impact on Peter. It has had a powerful impact on me, and I want to examine it together in depth.

As the story begins, Jesus and his disciples had just arrived by boat near one of the Galilean villages. A crowd gathered around him as he disembarked.

> Then one of the synagogue rulers, named Jairus, came there. Seeing Jesus, he fell at his feet and pleaded earnestly with him, "My little daughter is dying. Please come and put your hands on her so that she will be healed and live." So Jesus went with him. (Mark 5:22–24)

I can only imagine the excitement this created, with villagers excitedly telling each other, "Jesus is here! The famous miracle worker! He might perform a miracle before our eyes." As the news raced through the community, more and more people swelled the crowd walking up from the lakeshore.

The growing crowd pressed together in the narrow village streets. Among them was a woman who had suffered from a bleeding disorder for twelve years. She'd spent all the money she had on doctors but to no avail; her condition had steadily worsened. She hoped that by merely touching Jesus' clothes, she could be healed. She approached Jesus stealthily and reached out a hand. The moment she touched the hem of Jesus' garment, her bleeding stopped, and she knew she was healed.

Immediately, Jesus stopped the procession. Knowing that healing power had gone out from him, "He turned around in the crowd and asked, 'Who touched my clothes?'" (Mark 5:30). The puzzled disciples pointed out that the crowd was densely packed, that everyone was touching one another and being touched in the throng of people.

Yet Jesus still searched for the one who had touched him and been healed.

Why did he take the time to do this, to respond to this interruption? After all, he was hurrying to heal a little girl who was dying at the other end of the street. What could be more urgent than that? Why did he take time now to find out who had touched him?

Jairus, remember, had come up to Jesus openly and asked him to heal his daughter. But whoever had touched him, though possessing the faith to be healed, was either afraid or unwilling to ask. Something else was wrong. I suspect that Jesus stopped because he sensed a deep need that went beyond physical healing.

The poignancy of this story deepens when we consider why the woman was afraid to ask for what she desperately needed. An obscure provision of Jewish law held that a woman who suffered from ongoing bleeding was to be treated as "unclean" for as long as the discharge of blood lasted (see Lev. 15:25–30). She was to avoid other people lest she make them unclean also.

So, in addition to her sickness and her increasing poverty, this woman had been systematically isolated from society for years. She was forbidden to mingle in a crowd. If she were to approach Jesus at all, it had to be done in secret. Sick, poor, and isolated for twelve long years; no wonder that she felt valueless and lacked confidence to ask for what she needed.

Somehow, Jesus sensed from her furtive touch that this woman had emotional wounds that needed healing just as much as her physical disability. He stopped the procession to Jairus's house until she came forward. Read what happened next:

> The woman, knowing what had happened to her, came and fell at his feet and, trembling with fear, told him the whole truth. He said to her, "Daughter, your faith has healed you. Go in peace and be freed from your suffering." (Mark 5:33–34)

Jesus took the time to listen to the woman's whole story, as if no other needs were calling him. As he listened, Jesus understood that the woman needed to make sense of her suffering. He called her *daughter*, a word that is powerfully resonant for me; I, too, have a daughter. She has been the light of my eyes since the day she was born. Fathers and daughters share one of the closest, tenderest human relationships.

To underscore the importance of Jesus' use of this word, consider the fact that this is the only time recorded in the gospels when Jesus called someone daughter.

Next, Jesus says to the woman, "*Your faith* has healed you" (emphasis added).

In these few words, it is as if Jesus is saying: "Woman, you haven't been rejected or forgotten by God. No, you are his daughter, inexpressibly dear to him. I know it has felt as if you were all alone, but he has never left you, he has never ceased to love you, and he treasures the faith that you have held fast through all your years of suffering. And now, daughter, you have become a miracle worker: your faith has healed you."

I choke up every time I read this story. The tenderness Jesus shows, treating this elderly, sickly woman as a dearly loved daughter, helps me understand his tenderness for us all.

But there's another daughter in this story: Jairus's daughter, who is dying only steps away. Imagine Jairus's frustration at this interruption. Can you feel his agitation mounting as Jesus patiently listens while this woman tells him "the whole truth" about her twelve years of suffering?

As she finally finishes her story, messengers come from Jairus's home with the worst possible news: his daughter is dead. Jesus immediately turns to Jairus and says, "Don't be afraid; just believe" (Mark 5:36).

Together, they go on to Jairus's house, where Jesus performs an even greater miracle than healing a woman from chronic bleeding. He brings Jairus's young daughter back to life.

Here is the crux of this story for me: Do you think that Jesus knew ahead of time how this story would play out? Do you think he knew he would bring Jairus's daughter back to life? The text gives no indication that he knew. In my reading of the Gospels, it seems to me that Jesus was content to know only what the Father chose to reveal to him at any given time. I think we are meant to understand that Jesus was acting in faith, without foreknowledge of the outcome, when he stopped to learn who had touched his garment in the crowd and why.

When Jesus sensed that a furtive touch in a crowded street was a muffled cry for help, he stopped and responded, though an urgent need awaited him a few steps further on. He obeyed the Spirit's prompting, believing that his Father was able to handle any consequences that might come from his obedience, whatever they might be.

What does this mean for us? If we are to be alert for opportunities to do the good works that God has prepared in advance for us, we must be attentive to the people he brings our way. If this interrupts our plans or our agenda, God can take care of any consequences that follow. The question is: will we respond in the moment, or will we harden our hearts?

Ephesians 2:10 is one of the verses I pondered when I realized that my zeal for planning and reaching goals might cause me to dismiss a God-sent interruption. It reads, "For we are God's workmanship, created in Christ Jesus to do good works, which God prepared in advance for us to do." These opportunities don't always announce themselves, as when Jairus openly shared his need; sometimes they are evidenced by only a slight, furtive touch.

I've come to realize that there are wounded people all around us who hide their wounds due to shame or pride or a multitude of reasons. This has motivated me to be alert and attentive as I go through my days, so that I don't walk past anyone God has put in my way.

In Chapter 12, we explored the biblical command to pray without ceasing. Its practice centers on a continual awareness of God's presence, sensitivity to the Spirit's prompting, and a readiness both to listen and to pray for guidance as we go through our days. Observant sensitivity to those around me is one of the things I consistently pray for; I try to remember to pray before every encounter, even if I'm simply saying hello as I walk past someone I know.

As I've sought to cultivate a responsive heart, different practices have been helpful in different seasons. A number of years ago, I began a list of answers to prayer and other things I was grateful for. I spent time each Sunday thanking God for these things. I found that a posture of gratitude enabled me to go through my days with joy, despite the ups and downs of daily circumstances.

During another time, when I was grieving a loss, I felt the need to spend regular time in confession, which meant that I first needed to reflect prayerfully on habits of heart, mind, and action that were ugly in God's sight. I don't understand the connection between my loss and my need for confession, but I've learned I can trust God to guide me to what I need. I've often taken comfort in an insight that Paul shared in his letter to the church in Rome: "The Spirit helps us in our weakness.

We do not know what we ought to pray for, but the Spirit himself intercedes for us with groans that words cannot express" (Rom. 8:26).

So often, I don't know what I ought to pray for. It's a wonderful gift to realize that I don't need to know; I just need to pray.

In addition to being sensitive and observant, we must become people with whom others feel safe to acknowledge their woundedness. We must always be prepared to make time to listen while someone tells us "the whole truth" about their years of suffering.

With these concerns in mind, many years ago I adopted a decision rule for dealing with interruptions: if someone asks for my time, I say yes, without evaluating whether this is a *good* use of my time or even whether I have time to give. When I considered what it would mean if I brushed off someone whom God had brought to me, it seemed like a grave risk. I realized that I needed to always be ready to set aside my own schedule.

This was a difficult step for me. I have many responsibilities and schedule my time carefully. I wondered whether saying yes to everyone would mean that I would waste time in pointless attempts at relationships. I had vague fears of drowning in a sea of other peoples' troubles.

As it has turned out, my fears were groundless. Though on occasion I feel that my time with someone was not well spent, I usually know fairly quickly whether I am able to be helpful or not. If in doubt, I persist with the relationship; I've learned that I don't always know what is helpful to another person and what is not.

The number of relationships I maintain at any point in time is often high, which does take a considerable amount of time. However, I know God has used me in many of these relationships for good, not to mention the good he has brought into my life from many of these friends. And, for all I know, when I stand before him one day, I may learn that the most important fruit of my life hinged on one or more of these relationships.

Does that seem like an overstatement? Consider the story of Jonathan, the eldest son of Israel's first king, Saul. As the eldest, Jonathan was the crown prince, the heir to his father's throne; moreover, he had an evident gift for leadership. He was a military hero, and everything we know about Jonathan from the Bible indicates that he was loved by the people whom he led. In sum, he was a prince who was well prepared for the throne.

However, the reason Jonathan is remembered has nothing to do with those traits. We remember him because he took the time to mentor a teenage shepherd named David who came to his father's court. In time, David became Israel's greatest king. The glimpses we have of Jonathan and David's relationship portray Jonathan's powerful impact on David's development as a leader, soldier, and man of God.

There aren't many people whose names are remembered after three thousand years, yet Jonathan is on that short list. We remember him solely because of his friendship with this shepherd boy who became king.

I suspect that *many of us will be surprised when we stand before God and see our work from his perspective.* We are likely to realize that the good work he prepared in advance for us to do did not always seem significant at the time. If we allocate our time based on the world's standards of importance, we will often choose wrongly. We must cultivate hearts that are responsive to the Spirit's leading, so that we discern the "good works which God prepared in advance for us to do" as we walk through our busy days.

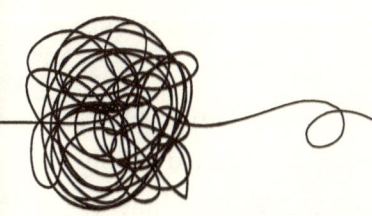

chapter seventeen

Leading a Quiet Life

*I*n Chapter 2, I referenced Charles Taylor's description of "the affirmation of ordinary life"[28] as a fundamental feature of Christian spirituality. We saw that Paul instructed the Thessalonian church to "make it your ambition to lead a quiet life, to mind your own business and to work with your hands, just as we told you, so that your daily life may win the respect of outsiders" (1 Thess. 4:11–12).

How we treat our family, neighbors, friends, and others is of prime importance. The good life is lived when we "live a life of love, just as Christ loved us" (Eph. 5:2), not when we achieve something in the public sphere that wins us praise.

We should focus our energies, then, on fulfilling our responsibilities—at work, in our parenting, in our marriages, and in our communities.

This notion runs counter to our cultural values. Americans don't want to be ordinary; they want to be special. Our culture pulses with messages about the supreme importance of fulfilling one's potential. There is a positive side to this emphasis: the creativity which American culture has unleashed, along with the broader thinking about human potential it has engendered, has amplified the church's timeless teaching about the dignity and unique value of every person.

But American culture is also distorted by selfishness. The truth about the potential and the value of each individual has been transmuted within American culture into an unhealthy obsession with personal fulfillment. This is particularly true with those outward markers of fulfillment that denote success.

Tolstoy begins *Anna Karenina* with these words: "Happy families are all alike, but unhappy families are each unhappy in their own way." The novel centers on two couples and the way their different choices unfold.

Anna, the title character, is one of the most appealing characters in fiction. Settled in a placid but unexciting marriage with an older man, she falls in love with a handsome young cavalry officer named Vronsky and eventually leaves her husband and son for him. Levin, the other central character, marries Kitty, who had been courted by Vronsky before he met and fell in love with Anna. Levin and Kitty build a home and raise children together; they build a durable happiness together, though it is not always easy and certainly not always exciting. Anna's choices end in misery.

Of course, the story Tolstoy is telling reflects the values of his day and time. Anna's values would seem to align better with our current culture than those of Levin and Kitty. And yet, were Tolstoy writing today, I doubt that his perspective would be different.

Tolstoy believed that marriage, though rooted in love between a man and a woman, had a more significant purpose than the fulfillment they can find in each other. That purpose is the family. Not all will marry; not all who marry will have children, and there are good reasons why one might choose the course of childlessness. But most of us will marry and follow God's injunction to Adam and Eve to "be fruitful and multiply" (Gen. 1:28 RSV).

Family provides each of us with an avenue for love—love that we give and love that we receive. Love often requires sacrifice, and there are times when self-fulfillment seems to be a better guiding principle for our lives than love.

Ironically, if self-fulfillment defines your purpose, you are very unlikely to find it, but if love defines your purpose, self-fulfillment is likely to follow. Jesus put it this way: "Whoever wants to save his life will lose it" (Matt. 16:25).

As a young man, I was confronted with my own distorted priorities. When I started setting goals for my life, more than thirty years ago, I spent a great deal of time thinking through my priorities, and I wrote them down. Fulfilling my responsibilities as a husband and father was at the top of my list. I still have that piece of paper.

My first child, Jack, was born on a Monday night. I brought Penny and Jack home from the hospital on Tuesday, and then I didn't see either of them again until Saturday.

My mother-in-law had come to spend the week with us, so I didn't leave my wife to fend for herself. Nevertheless, I left for work every day before they woke up and returned home every evening after they were in bed. I don't recall making it home before eight o'clock a single night that week.

I will never forget holding my son that Saturday morning, realizing that I had missed his first week of life, and recognizing that my actions were utterly inconsistent with what I had decided was most important to me. I saw that I needed to make major changes if my life was to reflect my priorities.

As I worked to make those changes, I came to understand that I had ingrained patterns of thinking and acting that stood in the way of change. Most of them were subconscious. I wasn't hypocritical, at least consciously, but I was naïve about how I made my decisions.

For example, I realized that I have an extreme bias for action and for completing whatever work is in front of me. If there's a task to be done, and I'm considering whether to work on the task or focus on an intangible, less urgent priority (such as spending quality time with my son), my nature is to gravitate toward the urgent, tangible task. I wouldn't characterize this approach as a weakness; it's simply a trait. It can have positive aspects, for I focus well, work hard, and accomplish a great deal. However, this decision process has nothing to do with living wisely; it cannot be trusted to produce the character I want.

I cannot rewire myself. Instead, I must have a realistic view of who I am if I want my life to center on the most important things. I came to realize that if I was going to live consistently with my values, I had to make intangible things tangible so they could compete effectively for my time and attention. Over time, I've learned to use my schedule to do just that.

While "spend quality time with my son" expresses a vague intention, "read to my son every night" is a task that I could put on my schedule. And I did. For this to happen, given his infant schedule, I had to be home by six o'clock. Therefore, this, too, became part of my daily routine. In other words, I developed a habit. In this case, the joy of spending time with my son was a powerful reward.

To sustain this habit, even given the obvious reward, I had to make a change. I had to perform my job within limited hours. To do this, I had to set priorities and be disciplined about pursuing them. I worked hard during my allotted hours, and I had to ensure that I was working on the most important things, or I wouldn't be able to fulfill my responsibilities at work.

I don't share these details with the idea that they are likely to prove helpful to you. The challenge posed by my distorted priorities was accentuated by my personality and my ambitions, things that are specific to me. I share them to illustrate that it's not enough to have a well-stated set of godly priorities. I had one of those, but my pursuit of those priorities was distorted by who I am and what I most wanted. Even realizing those barriers is not enough; I learned that I needed to take specific steps, every day, to create new habits if I was to live a godly life.

Work and family life are both important responsibilities for a follower of Christ. Together with our social relationships, they define how God intends us to live; they are at the center of the lives he designed us for, lives that enable us to participate fully in his plan for redeeming our world.

There are multiple ways to get off track. As Tolstoy said, "Unhappy families are each unhappy in their own way." I entered my adult years intent on fulfilling my career ambitions, and that priority presented many obstacles to godly living.

There are many other ways of living for ourselves. Some of us prioritize activities that give us pleasure, whether sports or social media or other things. I know others who continue to focus on earning as much money as they can, despite having long ago achieved wealth. I have other friends (and it's a temptation for me) who enjoy the prestige that comes with being a civic leader. Each of these assigns a higher priority to what I want for myself than to love. And even when we recognize that we have elevated the wrong priorities, that is not enough to bring about change. We must understand the way these priorities have become rooted in behaviors, in the way we plan and use our time, in the way we treat our friends and family members. Changing habits requires time and perseverance; I've found that it often takes as long as three years for me to consistently practice a new habit.

So much work can be involved in addressing matters that sometimes seem small. I remind myself of Paul's admonition to lead a quiet life. The responsibilities that are common to all of us are likely to prove more important than the things that make us "special."

chapter eighteen

Making Intentional Commitments

My generation has had access to a wider range of experiences than any generation before us. Steadily rising affluence continues to expand the breadth of possibilities for my children's generation, amplified by technologies that bring products, services, and knowledge closer to hand than ever before. At the same time, the removal of many types of moral constraints multiplies the options for satisfying our desires.

The lure of limitless choices is not a new development, though. More than eighty years ago, Reinhold Niebuhr wrote, "A technological civilization makes stability impossible . . . Its rapid developments and its almost daily changes in the physical circumstances of life destroy the physical symbols of stability and therefore make for restlessness . . . ."[29]

Many of the options presented to us by a wealthy and technologically advanced society are good; some are not. This has been true of the choices people have faced since the beginning of time. Whether you interpret the story of Adam and Eve literally or in some other way, the temptation posed by the forbidden fruit, which was "good for food and pleasing to the eye, and also desirable for gaining wisdom" (Gen. 3:6), has parallels in every human life that has been lived since.

The beckoning possibilities that surround us seem to promise great rewards: excitement, fulfillment, satisfaction, and maybe even wealth, honor, and praise. In a culture where we imagine that self-fulfillment is the most important task of life, those rewards seem worth every effort to pursue. And yet, very few find the rewards they anticipated. The joys of limitless choice are illusory. This, too, is an old, old story.

The writer of the biblical book of Ecclesiastes had enough wealth to indulge himself in every pleasure available, from building a personal empire to acquiring a harem. He writes, "I denied myself nothing my eyes desired; I refused my heart no pleasure . . . Yet when I surveyed all that my hands had done and what I had toiled to achieve, everything was meaningless, a chasing after the wind" (Eccl. 2:10–11). He advises us to enjoy our work; enjoy life with our spouses whom we love; enjoy simple pleasures like a good meal when hungry after a day of hard work; and "remember your Creator" (Eccl. 12:1). He ends with these words:

> Here is the conclusion of the matter: Fear God and keep his commandments, for this is the whole duty of man. For God will bring every deed into judgment, including every hidden thing, whether it is good or evil. (Eccl. 12:13–14)

As we have seen, all of us orient ourselves within a moral framework of our choice. This construct is an essential part of the identity we form as we grow and mature. Charles Taylor phrased it this way: "To know who you are is to be oriented in moral space, a space in which questions arise about what is good or bad, what is worth doing and what not, what has meaning and importance for you and what is trivial and secondary."[30] Without a moral orientation, we cannot make sense of who we are.

We have considered how Christian teaching marks a significant change in our understanding of what is important. The unique twist embodied in Christian spirituality involves what Taylor calls "the affirmation of ordinary life."[31] Taylor writes, ". . . the fulness of Christian existence was to be found within the activities of this life, in one's calling and in marriage and the family."[32] The crucial issue is how these activities are lived.

The framework upon which these choices rest consists of the individual commitments we make. The late Lewis Smedes wrote, "We are largely who we become through making wise promises and keeping them."[33] *Character is rooted in commitment.* Likewise, joy and meaning come from making the enduring commitments that life asks of us.

The allure of limitless freedom lies in its promise that a voyage of self-discovery is the essence of a life well lived. While we must learn to understand ourselves, identity is not lurking somewhere inside us, waiting to be discovered. Identity is not given to us at birth; it is something that we shape as we respond to life. We begin with certain resources and certain potential; these influence who we become, yet they are only part of the story. The rest is a function of the choices and commitments we make, how we make them, and whether we keep them.

Making commitments is one way in which we become unique individuals who rise above our "wiring," our social and cultural conditioning, and our training. We sometimes think of a commitment to one course of action primarily in terms of how it closes off other opportunities. But the freedom you feel while hesitating between choices is an illusion.

A commitment is an act of freedom. To quote Lewis Smedes again, "Only a person can make a promise. And when he does, he is most free."[34]

Until you choose, nothing is possible, since you cannot be in motion without choosing a direction. In contrast, immobility is a form of constraint, whether you are confined within walls or not.

Choosing frees you to explore a path that would otherwise be closed off to you. Yes, when you choose, you forgo other paths, which is why it is important to choose wisely.

We build character by making wise commitments as we engage in life. And the central importance of ordinary life means that the basics are the same for almost everyone.

If lasting joy comes from durable commitments and keeping faith, then the choices we make are important.

While some sets of choices lend themselves to being categorized as either good or bad, most choices involve aspects of both. Choosing requires trade-offs; we must weigh the positive and negative aspects of each possible choice so we can choose wisely. By implication, as we grow in wisdom and maturity, our decision-making will become more consistently good. But we will sometimes make a choice that has unanticipated consequences.

It would seem important, then, to make the *best* choice. When we choose, we cut off other options. What if one of those options proves to have been better than the option we chose? In a culture with a self-fulfillment ethos, we can imagine nothing worse. This can cause us to agonize over difficult decisions, wanting to be sure that we don't make a mistake. As a result, many people live suspended on the brink of commitment, paralyzed by anxiety about the choices they face.

Ironically, the teaching we receive in church often makes this anxiety worse. The prophet Isaiah wrote (I quote the King James Version (KJV) here, because I love the melody of its phrasing), "Thou wilt keep him in perfect peace, whose mind is stayed on thee; because he trusteth in thee" (Isa. 26:3). Beautiful words, and yet evangelical teaching sometimes magnifies anxiety rather than producing peace.

How many times have you heard a pastor say, "God has a perfect plan for your life." If that is the case, then of course we should strive to find that perfect plan. The implication of a "perfect" plan, though, is that any deviation is potentially disastrous. Young people pray for God to guide them; they want very specific guidance, because they wish to avoid making mistakes. But as every experienced Christian knows, God doesn't always guide us in a crystal clear way.

The reason for God's apparent reticence, as we have seen, is that God wants us to grow in wisdom. The Bible teaches that wisdom is the most precious of possessions, and that wisdom comes from seeing our experience through the lens of biblical truth. And experience consists of—mistakes.

Do you see the fallacy in the way we often think about this process? We want to make good decisions—nothing wrong with that, of course—and so we ask God to keep us from making mistakes. But mistakes play an essential role in our growth.

Here is a hard truth: *we should make and keep commitments even though we are likely to make mistakes in at least some of the commitments we make.* While the Bible doesn't say, "God has a perfect plan for your life," it does say, "In all things God works for the good of those who love him, who have been called according to his purpose" (Rom. 8:28). Though each of us makes mistakes along the way, God can bring good from any mistakes we make. Accordingly, we need to be ready to persevere when we commit to a choice that has unanticipated consequences.

Let's take a closer look at two of the commitments that define us—marriage and our church families. In Chapter 19 we will explore the role of friendships and other personal relationships, and in Chapter 20, the role of vocation.

Marriage

For those who marry, marriage is the central commitment of human life. I'm convinced that the decline in marriage rates in our country is largely responsible for the increasing turbulence, vulgarity, and dissatisfaction in our culture. This is not a judgment about any individual who chooses to be single. Paul wrote that God guides some people toward single lives, and he taught that singleness is a gift God gives, not a punishment.

Yet singleness today extends far beyond this group. According to a study by the Pew Research Center, for the first time in the modern era, young adults are more likely to live with their parents than with a spouse or partner. In 1960, 62 percent of eighteen- to thirty-four-year-old adults lived in their own households with a spouse. By 2014, only 31 percent did so, while 32 percent of this age group were still living with their parents.[35]

I shared my view of the teaching that God has a perfect plan for your life. Here is a similar teaching about marriage: God has a perfect partner designed just for you. If you believe this statement, let me ask this: *do you think anyone ever makes a mistake in choosing their marriage partner?* Wouldn't that mean that a man has just married someone else's perfect partner? In that case, not only have this man and woman damaged their lives, but they have also damaged the perfect partners that each of them was supposed to marry. And if those two go on to marry some less-than-perfect partner who happens to be available, the damage is multiplied. We can play this scenario out endlessly. If you work through the probabilities, I'm confident you'll find that even if there is a perfect partner for you, it would be mathematically impossible to find him or her.

Many people hesitate to marry because they are afraid of making a mistake. Often, that fear is accentuated by the experience of growing up in a broken home and knowing the pain that ripples through divorce. But you can never be certain about the person you marry. Stanley Hauerwas, an American theologian and ethicist, once said, "We never know whom we marry; we just think we do . . . The primary problem is . . . learning to love and care for the stranger to whom you find yourself married."[36]

Success in marriage is not a matter of finding the perfect person. There is no perfect person. What you need is an unshakable commitment to the imperfect person you marry.

I imagine that few farmers would argue that their land comprises the perfect farm. Every plot of land has limitations of soil and is subject to climatic conditions that create their own limitations. The farmer didn't acquire his farm because it was perfect but because it was available when he wanted to buy, or it was inherited through his family, or for some other reason that involved trade-offs, just as every other decision in life requires trade-offs. You don't need the perfect farm to be a successful farmer, though. What you need is to understand the land's potential and plant crops that can flourish under those conditions.

Likewise, not all marriages are created equal. Couples will discover that they have greater or lesser degrees of shared interests and compatibility in such areas as personality, personal habits, and beliefs. There is no perfect person to marry, so you need to adapt to the potentialities of the person you are with. After all, that's exactly what your spouse must do with you.

There are other myths prevalent in our society today regarding marriage; most center on the idea that self-fulfillment is the goal of marriage. If that premise is accepted, it follows that a relationship should be ended if it ceases to be fulfilling.

The biblical teaching on marriage contrasts sharply with this view. Early in the narrative that tells us about the creation of the world, its creatures, and humankind, the concept of marriage is introduced when God makes this observation: "It is not good for the man to be alone" (Gen. 2:18). God's solution was to form the woman from the man's own body. When Adam saw Eve, he exclaimed, "This is now bone of my bones and flesh of my flesh" (Gen. 2:23), and the passage concludes, in verse 24, "For this reason a man will leave his father and mother and be united to his wife, and they will become one flesh." From the beginning, the goal of marriage has been to create an unbreakable partnership.

This one-flesh life, if persevered in, can lead to fulfillment of a deeper and richer kind than selfish living ever can. We can reach this fulfillment because, when we are forced to confront our selfishness, we have the chance to see it for what it is and to break it apart. This process takes us in the opposite direction from pursuing self-fulfillment as our primary end. The decision to marry and the repeated decisions to persevere through the trials and difficulties that every marriage faces shape us into different people than we otherwise would have been. It is one of the primary ways that we build our character.

Interestingly, those who persevere in keeping their marriage commitments tend to be happier—even those with "unhappy" marriages. Linda J. Waite, a professor of sociology at the University of Chicago, conducted wide-ranging studies of the impact of marriage; her research is summarized in a book called *The Case for Marriage*.[37] One of her conclusions is that, in many cases, "staying together is the best solution if the marriage becomes unhappy."[38] You may disagree with this statement; please know that I am not rendering a judgment on your situation. Every circumstance is unique; just because a finding applies in "many cases" doesn't mean it applies in all cases. Nonetheless, it is worthwhile examining the research to see what we can learn from it.

Waite's book draws on the National Survey of Families and Households, for which thirteen thousand adults were interviewed in the late 1980s, then interviewed again five years later. Participants were asked to rate their marriage on a scale of one to seven, with a score of one being awful and seven being excellent. Of those who rated their marriage a one, only about 10 percent divorced during that time. Of those who stayed together over the five years, 87 percent said that their marriages were now good—either a six or a seven.

Dr. Waite also analyzed the data for everyone who ranked their marriage below average in the initial survey. Five years later, fully three-fifths of the couples rated themselves in the top two categories for marital satisfaction.[39]

> Dr. Waite noted, "One reason divorce is relatively high in our society is because now either person can leave, and we are more willing to leave than we used to be if we hit a bad patch. We're less likely to work it through. But there's evidence that dramatic turnarounds are commonplace. *They're the typical experience.*"[40] (emphasis added)

She further commented, "I'm not making a moral argument; I'm making a public health argument—what's good for you."

"What's good for you"—this isn't the typical lens through which we view God's commands. When we use the lens of our cultural assumptions, God's commands can seem arbitrary or old-fashioned. We don't always consider that they are better for us than the alternative.

When God provides guidance for how we should live, in effect he is telling us: "Here is the way you are designed. Here is the way I've designed relationships to work. *Live according to the design, and things will go better for you.*" We all know that when we use something in a different way than it was designed to be used, we end up with a poor result. That is what has happened to our culture with respect to how we practice marriage.

Every marriage has rough patches. If you consider leaving as an option, your marriage is less likely to survive when things get rough. But if you work through the rough patch, two things tend to happen. First, when you can resolve issues with your spouse, you arrive at a happier place in the relationship. Second, you grow in maturity by working through your problems, and your spouse has a person who is easier to live with, which makes both of you happier.

Growing in character makes you a better person and a more lovable person. The decision to commit is an essential ingredient. Decisions made in the moment tend to be influenced heavily by the emotions of the moment. In contrast, living out a commitment made beforehand enables you to respond well to pressures of uncertainty and heightened emotion. You can make the decisions that, in the calm of reasoned retrospection, you would want to have made.

Ironically, as I was completing the first draft of this chapter, my wife of thirty-five years told me that she wanted to end our marriage. I pushed back, and we had several conversations about whether to continue, but she was firm in her decision. I don't blame her for the failure of the marriage; after so many years together, responsibility must be shared equally.

I share this about my own marriage because I want to make clear that I don't write about the importance of a marriage commitment in a judgmental spirit. Not all marriages will last. However, I still believe that it is wiser to exclude divorce as an option than to leave it on the table. Yes, some marriages will end, even in the face of such commitment. Nonetheless, the Bible clearly shows us that marriage is intended to be a lifelong commitment. And, as we have seen, social science research supports the view that most people are better off persevering through their difficulties.

Church

Some people (mostly pastors) argue that you should never leave a church once you join. Staying with a church through good times and bad, just as you would with a marriage, is, in their view, always the right approach.

There is much to be said for this perspective. I think it's unwise to leave a church just because you find that you disagree with the pastor on an issue or you're dissatisfied with other attendees. Searching for the perfect church is bound to be a fruitless endeavor, but there is a certain kind of maturity that comes through living out a commitment to long-term relationships.

In general, I think it's best to stay rooted in your church, even if you go through a season where you are less satisfied than you were previously. I've been experiencing such a season myself in my long-term church home. Several years ago, we began to make a leadership transition to assure our ability to reach younger families.

Our senior leaders had all been roughly my age; now they are twenty years younger. We've achieved our goal; we continue to maintain a strong outreach to families with children in the home. However, because of the changes this leadership shift brought—in music, ministry focus, teaching styles, and content—many individuals and couples in their fifties and sixties have chosen to leave our church. At least half of my long-term friends have left in the past few years. Although I understand and sympathize with their decisions to leave, I have chosen to stay. I want our church to maintain its ministry in our community, and I know that a generational leadership transition must happen if the ministry is to remain vibrant. I have many opportunities for usefulness in my church. I see my personal satisfaction to be less important than the contribution I can make to the church that God led me to many years ago.

In the years since our church began its leadership transition, my oldest son and his wife brought two little boys into the world. My grandsons are growing up in the family-friendly church that our leadership transition enabled us to maintain. They are two of the hundreds of young children that our church reaches each week through its ministry to young families.

Of course, there can be appropriate reasons for changing churches. As we leave one season of life and enter another, the church that suited us during the earlier season doesn't fit our needs as well. For example, when we were first married, my wife and I attended a church with a vibrant group of young couples. We formed some close friendships, learned, and grew. After our first child was born, we found that the church's childcare was sorely lacking, and we moved to a church with more young families. In my experience, this is common. Any child growing up in our secular culture will find it challenging to nourish a living faith all the way through to maturity, and it's natural for parents to want to give their children the best spiritual grounding they can.

Other times, though, we may be in a certain habitual way of thinking about the role our church plays in our lives, and we may need to consider having a change of heart and entering a new season there. Some years ago, I was talking with a friend who attended an excellent church that I knew well. It was seeker-driven, and the Sunday worship services reflected the fact that many in attendance had little if any spiritual background or biblical knowledge. My friend told me that he and his wife had decided to leave the church because "they were not being fed" in the sense of hearing challenging sermons aimed at mature believers. I challenged him to consider whether "being fed" should be their priority at this time of life; they'd been fed all their lives and were well capable of feeding themselves. As we continued the conversation, it seemed to me that my friend's priority for his church experience was a pattern of thinking that no longer reflected a spiritual need. I suggested they consider whether God had placed them in this church to help feed new believers.

If you are now considering changing churches, ask yourself why. What is your goal? If your goal is to be used by God as he builds his kingdom, you may choose to stay even though the church provides less personal satisfaction than it did in the past. If your goal is to be part of a church that serves you, you may want to ask whether that is the right goal.

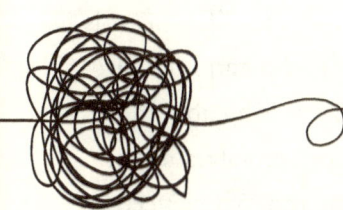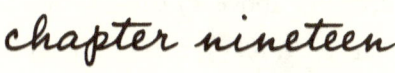
Making and Being a Friend

I suspect you overrate yourself. Most people do. I read recently that over 90 percent of American adults believe that they have above-average interpersonal skills. Over half rate themselves in the top ten percent. Think about the implications of those numbers. If interpersonal skills follow a normal distribution, no more than 30 percent of the population can possibly be above average. And I am hard-pressed to imagine how more than 10 percent of the population can squeeze into the top 10 percent.

In addition to deceiving ourselves about how pleasing we are to others, we take an equally rosy view of our intelligence and good looks, not to mention our more trivial attributes. Recently, a measurement taken during a routine physical exam forced me to see that I've been exaggerating my height for years. Not by much! But still.

You could argue that, in a sense, all this is harmless. If we're pleased with ourselves, we're probably better companions for our family, friends, and neighbors.

But even when we recognize that we've done something wrong, we are apt to rationalize it because we have the "inside scoop" on what impelled us to take that direction. When Jeremiah wrote, "The heart is deceitful above all things, and desperately wicked; who can know it?" (Jer. 17:9, KJV), this is at least part of what he was writing about.

We've established that every human being develops a moral framework. As we go through life and learn from both precept and experience, we develop values that express our personal views of right and wrong. For people to think well of themselves, they need to see that they are pursuing the right and the good within their moral framework. Because of this dynamic, we are all given to relentless self-justification. Even when we do wrong and know it, our need to see ourselves as "good" causes us to work hard to rationalize our shortcomings, either consciously or unconsciously.

This creates a real danger. I've come to believe that humility is the most important habit of mind that a person can have. We need to recognize that others have ideas, insights, and abilities that we lack; that we have blind spots; and that we easily deceive ourselves about what we do see.

This can pose a struggle if our natural habit of mind is to be satisfied with what we do and how we do it. Change is hard, and it usually begins with an unpleasant realization, giving us a motive to dismiss or deny challenges to our position or changes in the way we act.

This natural human drive highlights one reason why friendship is important. Who we are and who we become is powerfully influenced by the people we spend time with. They help to shape our wants, perspectives, habits, even beliefs. Furthermore, they help us see ourselves as we are; unless we have people in our lives who can be more objective about us than we can be about ourselves, we are likely to live with skewed perspectives.

The loneliness of American men has long been a cliché, but what the Surgeon General called the "loneliness epidemic" in a recent, widely publicized study, is not limited to men.[41] The study cites many contributing factors, including this startling statistic: since 1960, single-person households have grown from constituting 13 percent of the population to 29 percent. The study also shows that men and women tend to prioritize different things in relationships. When women feel lonely, they are 50 percent more likely than men to reach out to a family member or friend.

I've observed that men often take a more functional view of friendships. In church settings, they are as likely to seek accountability partners as they are to seek buddies. Women seem more oriented toward friendships that provide mutual support. The women's ministry in our church is almost an order of magnitude larger than the men's ministry, and I suspect this is not unusual. Friendship and accountability each have an important role to play, and relationships of varying kinds can be the source of both. Let's examine each in turn.

Friendship

While friendships naturally come and go, I wonder if widespread loneliness in American society is rooted at least partly in a lack of commitment. It's true that most friendships will be part of our lives for only a season, in contrast to the permanent commitment that comes with marriage. And yet a dimension of commitment is needed for our friendships to flourish.

A verse in Proverbs says, "There is a friend who sticks closer than a brother" (Prov. 18:24). If you have a friend like this, you know what a rich blessing it is. But to *have* a friend like that, you need to *be* a friend like that. I have found that committing to a friend brings rich rewards. I have been blessed with a few lifelong friendships formed during my high school and college years, and they have immeasurably enriched my life.

One such friendship is with a man who has been a close friend since middle school. In general, the longer someone knows you, the better their perspective on you. Friends from childhood or early adulthood, if you can keep them close, should have the best perspective of all. If you doubt that, ask yourself whether your siblings are impressed by you. Jesus commented, "Only in his hometown, among his relatives and in his own house is a prophet without honor" (Mark 6:4). There is a natural reason for this.

One challenge, of course, is that it's easy for friends to become distant in our mobile society. It's true that social media enables us to keep in contact with more people than ever, but that kind of contact tends to be less personal and not conducive to intimacy.

That middle school friend I referred to now lives within fifteen minutes of my home. For more than fifteen years, though, we lived in different parts of the country. We had to work at keeping in touch in the years before email, FaceTime, and social media, maintaining our friendship through letters, phone calls, and visits when possible. His friendship is one of the great treasures of my life. With him, I can always be—and am—completely open.

I have other long-term friendships that are not intimate but that are nonetheless a blessing to me. In the 1980s and early 1990s, my family and I lived in Southern California, followed by the Front Range urban corridor in Colorado, and then the Chicago area, roughly four years in each location. I continue to keep in touch with friends from each locale, though we settled in South Carolina more than thirty years ago. Long-term friendships, especially when founded on a common faith, provide both great joys and great benefits. It has taken effort to maintain friendships across the years and the miles, but it's been worth it.

One of those friendships is with a couple my wife and I got to know when we lived in Boulder in the late 1980s. In the more than thirty years that have passed since we moved away, I have seen this couple maybe half a dozen times. But Jim and I have corresponded consistently through all the years. We have not had the frequency of contact that would lead to intimacy. But the way Jim and his wife Katy have a radical commitment to obedience has always challenged me. I still remember a conversation where they shared their perspective on managing finances, for example. That conversation caused me to look at what the Bible taught about money in a different light and has had a powerful influence ever since.

Jim and I hold very different political views; temperamentally, he is an idealist who first asks, how should things be? I am pragmatic to the core, and my starting point is, what is realistic? His perspective will always challenge me; we often interpret events differently. Because we are so different, he is able to point out blind spots that mar my thinking. Because we are friends, I don't resent it when he does this; I know it comes from someone who loves me and who shares my commitment to following Christ.

I have found that, to be a good friend, I need to be purposeful and proactive in maintaining the friendship. Every year, as I set goals for the year ahead, I make a list of the relationships I want to maintain. As I go through the year, I usually plan my schedule a week at a time. Each week, I look at my relationship list and identify three or four friends and family members to reach out to. Sometimes it's a phone call; sometimes a note; sometimes I reach out to schedule breakfast or lunch. Consistently practicing the habit of connecting with friends and family each week keeps me from losing track of a friend inadvertently. For a friendship to flourish, it needs to be nourished by regular contact.

Almost every year, I realize that one or more relationships have come to an end. That's natural, and it frees up time and relational energy for the new relationships that are formed each year. To repeat, not all friendships are meant to endure beyond a season. We've all had friends who were in our lives for only a short period of time.

Some friendships have a narrower basis than others. My life has intersected with many people over the years—in work settings, while serving together in a church or ministry, or because we were neighbors. Most of these friendships didn't contain enough shared interests to keep the relationship going after that point of contact ended.

There are no rules for friendship, or for what commitment to a friend requires of us. I would simply advise you to be a good friend to your friends. Live a life of love among them. "Be kind and compassionate to one another, forgiving each other, just as in Christ God forgave you" (Eph. 4:32).

Accountability

Seeking accountability is the foundation for a posture of humility. When you take this step, you acknowledge that you are a flawed person and that without outside help you will wallow in sinful attitudes, thoughts, desires, and actions that will stunt your growth. Becoming a person of humility begins with the attitude of the heart, but it must be expressed in concrete action to be completed.

When we allow ourselves to be morally "naked" in front of a trusted friend and ask for help, we acknowledge the truth about ourselves.

I cannot overemphasize the importance of this step. Pursuing intimacy in a relationship is a powerful test of our integrity. Is our goodness rooted within us, or is it a façade that hides secret places in our hearts? Are we content to present ourselves as people of character, or are we willing to do the hard, humiliating work needed to possess character and to be good through and through?

Sadly, healthy accountability relationships are rarer than they should be.

Over the years, I've worked closely with highly successful people in business, government, and ministry. Some fell suddenly and in very public ways. Others drifted off their course and gradually lost their impact or credibility.

The biblical record confirms this observation. The Bible depicts many leaders who went off track, sometimes after years of success and, at least apparently, godly living. Many of us are familiar with the failures of David and Solomon, but countless other leaders failed to finish as well as they began—Samuel, Uzziah, Hezekiah, Josiah, Joash, and more.

Successful people share a common affliction: they are surrounded by people who are vying for a place at their side. The more successful one becomes, the more of these people there are. The world is filled with people who crave an association with success—for some, because it's exciting; for others, because they're pursuing access to money or power; while still others are seeking the ego gratification of being associated with success (do you know any name-droppers?). Because they want to protect their insider status, these people have a powerful motive to tell their successful friend exactly what they want to hear.

After a while, the inner circle of many successful leaders is composed primarily of these status-seekers, because eventually they push everyone else aside. When this happens to a leader, everyone around them does nothing but affirm, tell them how brilliant and good they are, and admire their every word and action. When everyone around you tells you how wonderful you are, it's natural to believe it.

While leaders may face this vulnerability to a higher degree, it is a challenge for each one of us. We all tend to surround ourselves with people with whom we are comfortable, who don't challenge us. The sad upshot is that, from what I've seen, not many people finish well. This is important, whether or not we think of ourselves as leaders. Each of us affects every life we touch—in our homes, the places where we work, the neighborhoods we live in, our churches, and so on. Each of us has a deceptive heart. If we are to see ourselves accurately, we need the help of others.

My pastor and long-time friend, Greg Surratt, who founded Seacoast Church in Charleston, South Carolina, is fond of saying that we need people close to us who love us but are not impressed by us. True friends care more about us than they do about anything they could receive from us. But people like this will not fight for a place at your side. To keep them close to you, you need to be purposeful about holding them close.

Not all friends are well-suited to be accountability partners. I have friends whom I would never ask for critical feedback because they're not the kind of people who like to give it—they're hardwired to affirm and encourage rather than express the hard truths that we sometimes need to hear. While affirmation and encouragement are important for all of us, they are generally not sufficient to nourish personal growth.

Some relationships will be narrowly focused, while others will be broader. For example, I have several coaching relationships with younger professionals who have recently become, or are in the process of becoming, executive leaders in the company or ministry where they work. We connect regularly to discuss the whole range of issues that come with that role, from analytical frameworks to best use of time, to leading and advising with integrity. Some are fellow believers, and some are not. None of them, though, share a comprehensive picture of their lives with me. They are simply seeking to access learnings from my professional experience in the hope that this can help them become the leaders they seek to be.

Accountability tends to work best when it is mutual, in other words, when two or more people agree to hold each other accountable for a common area or areas of their lives. There can be exceptions, of course; in the relationships I just described with younger professionals, the accountability flows primarily one way. This is often the case with mentoring relationships. When a younger person approaches someone with more experience in an area where they need accountability, they may feel that they have little to offer the more experienced person. These relationships can work, though they tend not to last as long, because asymmetrical relationships can't go as deep. The key in either case is to be clear about what role you are inviting the other person to play in your life.

It's important to be clear about the ground rules surrounding transparency. If I ask someone to hold me accountable in an area of my life, or for us to hold each other accountable, we need to discuss what level of transparency we will commit to and how we will share that information.

On more than one occasion, people have asked me to hold them accountable in an area of life, and it quickly became apparent to me that what they really wanted was affirmation, not accountability. Transparency is critical for an accountability relationship to be helpful, and you must agree ahead of time on what that means. Otherwise, you will quickly run into an issue where you don't want to tell your accountability partner the truth, or at least the whole truth, which defeats the purpose. Not only do you fail to receive the feedback that fuller disclosure would make possible, but you also damage trust, which inhibits the relationship's development. In my experience, unless you set clear expectations about transparency ahead of time, it is probable that when temptation comes you will rationalize withholding information. And if you do that, you set yourself up to undercut the very benefits that such a relationship has the potential to bring.

At the same time, accountability relationships should not be fundamentally confrontational. Transparency and vulnerability can only flourish within a covering of trust. You must know that the person from whom you are seeking accountability is someone who loves you, genuinely wants the best for you, and is wise enough to help you discern it. Otherwise, you are vulnerable to spiritual abuse.

Accountability, then, is rooted in support rather than confrontation. Even when rebuke is necessary and appropriate, its goal is always restoration and spiritual growth.

Small groups have flourished in the Western church since John Wesley introduced them in the early days of Methodism, more than 200 years ago.[42] Many Christians continue to join short- or long-term groups for this blend of support and accountability, as well as providing a forum for group study, service projects, or other focal points.

I encourage you to take some time to reflect so you can assure that friendship and accountability have their proper place in your life. Remember our quote from Jeremiah at the beginning of the chapter: "The heart is deceitful above all things." There are few aspects of life where we are more liable to self-deception than our need for intimacy. I sometimes think this is Satan's method of ensuring our mental and moral complacency. If we are complacent, we are vulnerable to fall, as so many of us do during the course of life. I've seen many falls from which there was never a full recovery. Nothing is more important if you want to "run with perseverance the race marked out for [you]" (Heb. 12:1).

Begin by making an inventory of your friendships. What important areas of your life do they cover? Are you investing enough time for them to be effective? Like a garden, your friendships will flourish only if they receive attentive care. If the relationship is primarily focused on accountability, is there a shared understanding of the dimensions of accountability that the relationship is to uphold? What does this inventory show you? What gaps do you see?

As you think about these gaps, think also about your attitude toward transparency with others. Any area of your life that you keep hidden—that you allow no one to see, much less speak into—is a spiritual risk, not to mention a risk in practical terms. Americans prize autonomy, but uncorrected it can lead to disaster.

Is there anyone in your life who confronts you when you are wrong? Is there anyone you have allowed to get close enough to know when you are wrong? If not, then you have structured your life to deny yourself the information you most need. It's a comfortable way to live, which is why so many of us gravitate toward it. But it may prove fatal to your most cherished hopes.

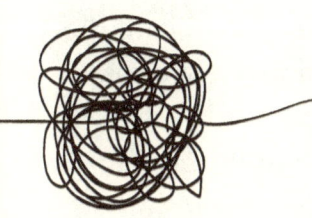

chapter twenty

Working as Unto the Lord

My father worked his entire thirty-nine-year career for a single company. Few in my generation have had that opportunity, and there may be even fewer such opportunities awaiting my children and their peers in the years ahead. The pace of change in the workplace, accelerated by the competitive forces brought to bear by economic globalization, has increased the rate at which companies are born, mature, and either fade away or are swallowed up by other firms. Considering this environment, what does godly behavior look like in the sphere of work and career? What should we strive for?

While we can't predict or control how long our current employment relationship will last, we can control our commitment to it while we are there. The writer of Ecclesiastes provides this pithy advice: "Whatever your hand finds to do, do it with all your might" (Eccl. 9:10). Paul affirms this viewpoint, and adds a twist:

Whatever you do, work at it with all your heart, as working for the Lord, not for men, since you know that you will receive an inheritance from the Lord as a reward. It is the Lord Christ you are serving (Col. 3:23–24).

We should work hard, because every job is ultimately done for the Lord. He is the one we are serving, and he is the one who will reward us. Those of us who work in business and government don't always think of ourselves as doing spiritual work, yet we serve Christ through our work just as much as those who are called to service jobs and ministry.

Our work itself is of intrinsic value. The Genesis account describes God himself performing the work of creation, seeing that it was good, and resting from his work. He charged Adam and Eve with responsibility to steward the earth and its plant and animal life; he "took the man and put him in the Garden of Eden to work it and take care of it" (Gen. 2:15). Each community must work cooperatively to provide food, clothing, shelter, transportation, and other needed things. Each of us who is able to work has a responsibility to carry our share of the common load. I long ago realized that the primary way I serve others is through my work, not my so-called ministry activities.

Serving others in love is central to God's will for each of us, whether the setting for our service is ministry or the marketplace. I read an essay yesterday in one of the national news outlets. The writer, an attorney, was hurrying through an airport to his connecting flight. Seeing a shoeshine stand, he remembered that his shoes were badly scuffed, and he took a seat. As he sat there, his mind wandering among many things, his attention was gradually drawn to the young man shining his shoes. The young man was completely focused on his work, which he performed with evident skill and unhurried care. His attentive, personal service was felt as a gift by the attorney, as a hand extended across the divide that usually separates us from other human beings. The job was a small thing, completed in a few moments, but it was invested with all the meaning that those moments could carry.

Our work gives witness to our faith, always through actions and sometimes through words, and reaches many people who may never talk to a pastor.

I once heard a Christian business leader share a formative experience from his early career. He was a relatively new business owner at the time and was eager to use his business as a platform for ministry. One day, during a conversation with a supplier, he saw an opening to talk about spiritual matters and began to share his faith. The supplier, an older man, cut him off abruptly with these words, "I'd have a lot more interest in what you have to say if you paid your bills on time." The young man was stunned into silence. He had not connected his ability to be a witness for Christ with his own business practices.

In my experience, anyone in the workplace who is known to be a Christian is scrutinized closely. While some people may simply want the chance to discredit anyone who professes faith, others—and these are the majority, I am convinced—are watching to see if their faith is real. They want to identify whether anything is *different* about the life of someone who believes. As Paul wrote, "The creation waits in eager expectation for the sons of God to be revealed" (Rom. 8:19). Doing our work as unto the Lord is one way that we provide glimpses of the future God invites us to share, in hope "that the creation itself will be liberated from its bondage to decay and brought into the glorious freedom of the children of God" (Rom. 8:21).

Does your work life hold up under such scrutiny? And, if your public face is "clean," what about the thoughts and actions that no one sees?

I love the picture that is painted by Proverbs 28:1: "The wicked man flees though no one pursues, but the righteous are as bold as a lion." If your actions are leavened with any trace of dishonesty, you will always be sensitive to the risk of discovery. You will be cautious when the times call for boldness; you will be fearful in interpreting unforeseen responses by family, friends, and co-workers; and you will be over-protective of your vulnerabilities when contesting a point of principle or policy.

On the other hand, the knowledge that you have nothing to hide from anyone enables you to be as bold as a situation demands. Therefore, *commit not only to doing your best but to working with absolute integrity.*

There is a longer-term dimension for most of us as we consider our vocational commitments. While you can achieve a certain measure of excellence in your work by doing your best today, most types of work contain opportunities for growth in skill and knowledge. And the Bible contains much teaching about our responsibility to grow continually through life.

The central text of this book, 2 Peter 1, teaches that we should seek to grow continually in the qualities of character it enumerates: "Make every effort to *add to* your faith goodness; and to goodness, knowledge . . . For if you possess these qualities *in increasing measure*, they will keep you from being ineffective and unproductive in your knowledge of our Lord Jesus Christ" (2 Pet. 1:5, 8, emphasis added).

This doesn't mean that everyone should set high goals in their chosen or current career. Work and career have different relative importance for different people. To some, work is primarily a means of earning the money they need to support other things. The focus of their personal growth will probably lie in other areas of their lives. For example, in young families, it often happens that one parent is the primary breadwinner, and the other parent works to supplement the family's income, often part-time. The parent with the part-time role may not work in an area of long-term interest; therefore, the long-term importance of this kind of work in their life is likely to be considerably less than for others.

God does want us all to commit to some path of growth and meaning as we go through our lives. Each person's path is unique, and there are no rules, only biblical principles that we should seek to embody wisely in our lives.

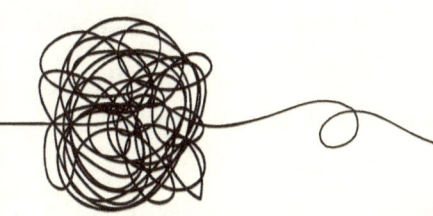

chapter twenty-one

Working for Justice

We often assume that we fulfill the command to "love your neighbor as yourself" (Lev. 19:18; Matt. 19:19) through our personal relationships, whether they are close and intimate or spring from single encounters. But there is a broader dimension to that command. We are charged to serve those who have been disadvantaged by the society we live in, to "speak up for those who cannot speak for themselves, for the rights of all who are destitute" (Prov. 31:8).

The man or woman who follows this process can have great impact, not only in their personal relationships but also in their broader involvements. In his classic book *Servant Leadership*, Robert Greenleaf wrote that one's pursuit of the good should include "effective involvement with the ethical dilemmas of one's times."[43] I believe that working toward societal justice is an important dimension of loving our neighbors. Social justice is one of the dominant themes of the prophetic books in the Bible, particularly Isaiah, Amos, and Micah. While fair and consistent application of the Law is commanded for those who administer it, the scriptural resonance of justice goes much further by invoking right-dealing, while protecting the weak, the powerless, and the outsider.

There is no doubt that obedience to God requires that we serve other people. It is how we fulfill Jesus' command to love our neighbors. This love is not merely a matter of words but of action, as John points out: "Let us not love with words or tongue but with actions and in truth" (1 John 3:18). Love is built on faith, through which we believe in a God who can provide all our needs; he is also able to give us the time, wisdom, resources, and anything else we need to complete the work he has assigned us. This principle applies to being generous with time as much as it does to being generous with money.

I am not one who sees only injustice when they view American society. Certainly, injustice is present, just as injustice has been embedded in every society that has ever been formed. The primary responsibility of civil government is to establish and maintain order, and any such system designed and administered by fallible human beings will embody injustice to a greater or lesser extent. And sometimes leaders and other decision-makers must make a choice in a setting where there are no good options; a degree of injustice may be part and parcel of the least bad option available to them.

To realize these truths is not to endorse a resigned acceptance. We cannot eliminate injustice, but we can lessen it and soften the impact of the injustice that remains. If one of the distinctive failings of our society is the failure of its institutions, many of us will need to be engaged in institutional life, working to increase the capacity of those institutions to mediate love.[44]

As we do so, we must remember that those with the power to shape society's choices become corrupted by that power in one way or another and thereby corrupt our society. People who are part of more privileged groups are unlikely to see the injustice that their privilege inflicts on those outside the group. *Privilege itself distorts one's perspective.*[45]

A verse from Proverbs has haunted me ever since I first read it many years ago: "If a man shuts his ears to the cry of the poor, he too will cry out and not be answered" (Prov. 21:13).

It's easy to justify myself based on a literal rendering of that phrase. I don't remember hearing poor people cry out for help and ignoring them. But then, I am fortunate enough to have lived in safe, affluent suburban enclaves. I don't have regular contact with poor people in the normal course of my days, whether at my place of work, when shopping, or walking through the neighborhood.

What does it mean to shut your ears to the cry of the poor if you live in an environment whose very structure keeps the poor at a distance? Just because I don't hear their cry doesn't mean that poor people aren't out there. At some point, I realized that if I am to hear the cry of the poor, then I need to go where they are.

For several years I served as a board member for a provider of services to homeless people in my home city. It was a great opportunity for me to use my talents and skills to help people in need.

However, I also learned through my years on the board that it's important for me to serve more directly with people and in ways that may not use my professional skills. For years I served on teams that prepared and served meals in a soup kitchen. Many of the faces I saw were not the stereotypical faces of homelessness that we may imagine— drug-wasted, toothless, and prematurely aged. Instead, they looked as capable, energetic, and intelligent as any other group in our society.

They were people who looked much like me.

As I learned more about homelessness, I came to see that the difference between those who end up in a shelter and those who don't often doesn't depend on talent, hard work, or accomplishment. More often, it hinges on whether a person has a support network in place that can help them get back on their feet when they stumble. My work with the homeless came on the heels of my wife Penny's extended illness and bone marrow transplant. As I mentioned earlier, I came to realize how much the apparent stability of our home had depended on the support we received from our extended family, our church family, and others.

We all stumble; we all experience challenges that are too great to overcome on our own. We are all vulnerable, and oftentimes we don't see our vulnerability until it's too late. At the same time, all of us have an inherent dignity that is to be respected and defended.

It is natural for prosperous people to think well of themselves and justify their privileges as a reward for their hard work and "clean" hands. However, we are no better than our brothers or sisters in the shelters across the land. Spending time at the shelter, serving people who have no choice but to acknowledge their need and seek assistance, helped me to remember the weakness embedded in human nature that I, too, carry. When I hear the cry of the poor, I remember my own vulnerability.

Just as it is a matter of obedience to make time for the individuals whom God brings into my life, working for justice is also a matter of obedience. In my experience, it is an aspect of life that looms ever more important as I seek to live faithfully and humbly.

Humbling ourselves is not equivalent to self-abasement. Rather, when we humble ourselves, we see, in their true proportions, those things that are bigger than we are. This is true of God. It is also true of the immense, beautiful, variegated, suffering world in which he has placed us and where he gives us the opportunity to serve. And, as we see these things in their true proportions, we have another vantage point from which to see ourselves, our motives, and our actions.

Our life choices may seem perfectly appropriate and fully obedient to biblical teaching within the context of our circle of personal relationships, which is likely constituted by people with similar backgrounds and other shared resemblances. However, those choices may be less adequate when viewed from a broader perspective.

For example, if God has blessed you with wealth and you give a portion of your income to the church and other ministries that is comparable to the giving of your Christian friends, does that reflect obedience? Maybe it does. But it is possible that God will challenge you to give beyond your comfort level when you consider the needs of those around you. For those of us with wealth, the question is not how much we should give but how much God wants us to keep for ourselves when people he loves are hungry, lack shelter, and are unable to provide for their families, and when there are millions of people in our world who have never heard the gospel.

Let me caution you: working for justice is likely to prove frustrating at first, and maybe for an extended time. Identifying injustice is easy, but it is difficult to make things better.

A few weeks ago, I read an article about an ambitious program, funded by one of the world's leading philanthropists, aimed at enabling more talented, low-income students to attend top-flight colleges and universities. Bloomberg Philanthropies has invested over $140 million in this project over the span of a decade, working with a group of college presidents whose schools share the same goals.

What did the program accomplish? Virtually nothing. As they've measured outcomes, they found that 51 percent of students with access to the program enrolled in high-graduation-rate colleges; a control group with no such access had a 50 percent enrollment rate.

Government-funded poverty programs have a similar record. In 1974, within a few years of the War on Poverty programs initiated by the federal government, 16.1 percent of households had income levels that were below the federal poverty rate. Fifty years and trillions of dollars later, 14.7 percent of households fell below the threshold. When you account for the imprecision with which we measure poverty, there is likely no statistically significant difference in outcomes.

As a society, we have striven mightily to find scalable, cost-effective strategies to solve enduring societal problems. With a few exceptions, we have had a notable lack of success.

This is not a conservative attack on government poverty programs, nor a progressive attack on billionaire philanthropy. But the resources such programs provide, though necessary, are not sufficient to solve deep-rooted human problems. To be effective, such programs must be combined with another resource: personal, relationship-building time.

Some years ago, I met a young man in the process of starting a staffing business whose purpose was to help homeless people achieve permanent employment and become financially self-sustaining. Our meeting came as I was completing my board service with the homeless services provider. I'd seen what a barrier temporary employment could be (you may not realize this, but most homeless people are employed, they simply don't earn enough to afford housing). I thought, *if we could solve this problem, it would make a big difference.* I supported the young man as he went through the start-up phase and ended up becoming his business partner.

During the years we were partners, we helped well over one hundred men and women achieve permanent employment. Sadly, this was a small fraction of the people we worked with. We were helping remove one obstacle, but most of our workers faced other obstacles too. Each person had their own story. To help, you had to know their story, which meant you had to be trusted. Trust can be hard to win from members of groups who feel marginalized by the broader community.

I also saw that these personal obstacles often hardened into habits of mind as well as action. The biggest obstacles facing many of our workers were their own assumptions about what was possible for them and what was not.

It was as though these men and women were restrained by a lock they couldn't open, and you had to find the specific key for each lock to help someone be free. Even more, once free, most people needed support to stay free. Our habitual ways of thinking don't automatically change when circumstances change; people need ongoing support to help them develop the habits of thought and action that sustain freedom.

This kind of support isn't scalable. It happens one person at a time.

Similarly, researchers studying the Bloomberg education initiative found that providing access to resources did little for the students they wanted to help. What helped was in-person counseling.

In our churches, when we encourage generosity, we usually talk about money. Giving financially is good and necessary—it provides resources that can underpin others' freedom while helping us become free as well. The command to "keep your lives free from the love of money" (Heb. 13:5) applies even more to givers than receivers.

But what about our time? As a busy young careerist, I thought I could simply give financially and let other, less busy people invest their time. Specialization! But I came to see that hoarding my time was just as ruinous as hoarding money.

I'm in a season of life—children raised, winding down my career— where I have much freedom in directing my time. A parent juggling work and the needs of young children has much less freedom, sometimes none. And yet, even when you are in such a season, consider whether there is life-on-life engagement that is possible for you.

It's not just the rich whom God invites to give of their financial resources; it's a faith step that applies to everyone. In the same way, I think that some avenue of service is desirable for everyone. Ours is a culture that lends itself to self-absorption; all of us are more self-absorbed and self-protective than we realize. To combat our culture's comfortable messages, we need to ask, what does it mean to "live a life of love, just as

Christ loved us and gave himself up for us" (Eph. 5:2) as Paul instructs us to do?

I don't know the answer to that question, but I'm convinced that I need to keep asking it. Not long ago, a friend shared a need with me—not his own need but another person's. My initial thought was: *this is not realistic for me to take on.* My friend wasn't even asking me to take it on. He was just telling me about it because he felt he ought to tell me. As I prayed about what to do, or whether to do anything, the thought occurred to me, *If not me, then who?* I couldn't think of anyone else. And though the scope of the need exceeded my resources, it didn't exceed God's.

It's easier for me to turn away from a situation like this than to turn toward it. I remind myself of a verse we have examined before, something the writer of Hebrews repeats three times: "Today, if you hear his voice, do not harden your hearts" (Heb. 3:7-8, 15; 4:7).

Let me encourage you to be one of those people who perseveres in doing good.

Do not give up.

Listen for the cries of the poor.

To quote Galatians 6:9 again: "Let us not become weary in doing good, for at the proper time we will reap a harvest if we do not give up."

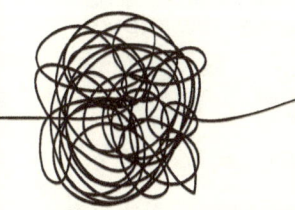

Closing Words

A few weeks ago, I had a long conversation with a man with whom I attended graduate school. We hadn't talked in the more than forty years since our graduation.

As we talked, Dan asked about my faith journey—he was struck by something I'd posted on LinkedIn that referenced my faith. He said, "I didn't remember that in the guy I knew . . ." He didn't complete his thought, but he didn't need to; I certainly wasn't living for Christ in those years.

And yet my years in graduate school were a time of considerable spiritual ferment and growth for me. During my senior year in college, I realized that I hadn't accepted my parents' beliefs, but I hadn't rejected them either. I read through the Bible that year so I could decide which way to turn. Over the course of the year, I became convinced that the Bible was God's Word, that Jesus was who he claimed to be, and that belief in him and his saving work on the cross was the basis for salvation. I accepted the Christian faith as my own, not simply something I'd grown up with. Yet it took years of spiritual journey for God's work to become visible in my life, a process that has continued—slowly, sometimes joyfully, and often painfully—in all the years since.

The evangelical churches in which I've spent my adult life focus primarily on leading spiritual seekers to the point of decision, accepting Christ as their savior and Lord. I appreciate the importance of this work, but, in this context, when we celebrate spiritual growth, it is most often baby steps that we are celebrating.

A few years ago, our pastor interviewed a Christian business leader on the platform, rejoicing in this leader's stated vow to "give his company to Christ." I remember thinking, "Now it begins for you, my friend." The businessperson's step wasn't a culmination but a beginning; having acknowledged that Christ was the Lord of his business, he would now face the myriad challenges of discerning how to live out his commitment hour to hour and day to day.

Everyone who seeks to follow Christ faces the same set of challenges: how to live out our faith in the ordinary material of daily life. We have family members, friends, and neighbors to love; time and energy to allocate wisely; and money to manage.

We also need to recognize the forces that will impede our progress. Some are within—sin, habit, complacency, even unbiblical assumptions that we are not conscious of. Other forces are external, including cultural expectations and spiritual opposition in all its forms. These forces are not defeated at a moment in time, but gradually, step by step, as we move forward on the path of life.

As a parent and now, a grandparent, I enthusiastically celebrate baby steps. This is because these steps begin the journey to the lifetime of maturity that lies ahead. We are wise to recognize that baby steps occur much closer to the starting line than to the finish line.

Paul admonishes us to "live a life worthy of the calling you have received" (Eph. 4:1). The writer of Hebrews expresses the same exhortation with a metaphor: "Run with perseverance the race marked out for [you]" (Heb. 12:1).

No one learns to run without first learning to walk, first taking baby steps. And even experienced runners stumble and fall. The whole process is humbling, and that is as it should be. Paul continues in Ephesians 4:2, "Be completely humble and gentle; be patient, bearing with one another in love."

I hope this book has provided glimpses of the path to maturity that lies ahead—beyond baby steps—to run the race marked out for you. I hope it has encouraged you to run *your* race with perseverance in the face of obstacles.

As you pursue your path toward godly living, seek to replace established habits with new ones, complete with rewards to reinforce them. Make your goals manageable and be patient with yourself.

As you do these things, maintain a responsive heart, one that is open to new work that God has for you. One of my favorite verses is Hosea 10:12:

Sow for yourselves righteousness, reap the fruit of unfailing love,
and break up your unplowed ground; for it is time to seek the
Lord, until he comes and showers righteousness on you.

While it is good to sow in the places and in the ways that we are accustomed to sowing, we also need to challenge ourselves to go beyond what we know, to break up unplowed ground in our lives. God will expand our harvest as we bring every area of life under his cultivation. Don't wait to obey his voice until you feel ready, "for *it is time* to seek the Lord."

Above all, remember that you are not expected to accomplish this on your own.

In Philippians 1:6, Paul assures us that "he who began a good work in you will carry it on to completion until the day of Christ Jesus."

John Henry Newman, whom I quoted in chapter 1, framed this point succinctly: "It is but building on the sand to profess to believe in Christ, yet not to acknowledge that without him we can do nothing."[46]

Let me close by once again sharing Peter's challenge to you and me:

Make every effort to add to your faith goodness; and to goodness, knowledge; and to knowledge, self-control; and to self-control, perseverance; and to perseverance, godliness; and to godliness, brotherly kindness; and to brotherly kindness, love. For if you possess these qualities in increasing measure, they will keep you from being ineffective and unproductive in your knowledge of our Lord Jesus Christ (2 Pet. 1:5–8).

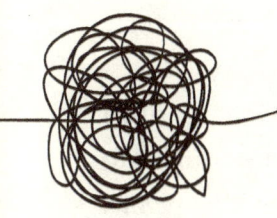

Acknowledgments

The catalyst for this project was a question posed by lifelong friends Chuck and Nancy Snyder, in a letter written in 2014: "Of all the things you would like to do with whatever earthbound years remain—what rises to the top of the pile?" Thank you, Chuck and Nancy, for decades of encouragement, prayer support, and spiritual sharpening.

My best friend for more than five decades, Paul Heinauer, provided helpful comments on an early draft and unfailing support and encouragement through the years that this project has taken. My sincere thanks to other readers of draft manuscripts: Jenna Surratt, Linda Herman, Nick Johnston, Darrin Patrick, Joe McKeown, Sue Reed, Nancy Hoey, Scott Edmondson, Matthew Palmer, Joey Svendsen, Ray Ferrell, Chris Taylor, Andi Andrews, and Barton Swaim. Your insight and encouragement were a great gift, and I wouldn't have completed this work without it.

Bonnie Budzowski worked with me for more than a year to put this book in final form. Bonnie, your editorial skill and spiritual wisdom enabled a far better result than I could have achieved without you. Jenn Freemon and Nate Schaub of Mindflint were great design partners for the cover and website. My brother Dan connected me with both Bonnie and the Mindflint team.

Jack, James, and Park—as I have worked to express the spiritual lessons I learned from Poppy, I have thought continually of you and your families. I couldn't be more grateful to God for your presence in my life.

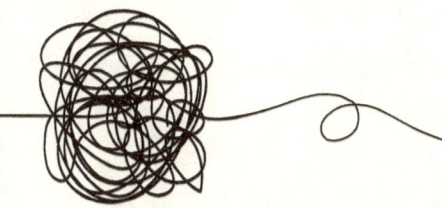

About the Author

*J*ack Hoey brings a lifelong commitment to integrity, servant leadership, and spiritual formation across business, ministry, and public service. Over a career spanning decades, he has held executive roles in both corporate and nonprofit settings, always guided by his Christian faith.

Jack served as chief financial officer of Stevens Towing Co., Inc., a diversified maritime firm, from 2014 to 2025, while leading a management consulting practice that advised small and midsize companies in industries ranging from heavy manufacturing to cloud services. Earlier in his career, Jack led an investor group in acquiring Coastal Glass Distributors, serving as its president for nearly fourteen years and transforming it into a nationally respected fabricator of architectural glass. Under his leadership, the company earned multiple honors for growth and workplace culture.

Alongside his work in industry, Jack devoted significant energy to ministry. He played foundational roles at Seacoast Church—a multi-site congregation with average attendance exceeding 15,000—serving as its first board chair (2001–2010) and later as executive director of operations. His commitment to the local church remained steadfast; after retiring from staff in 2019, he returned as board chair from 2020 to 2023. Jack has also provided long-term leadership to the global mission organization Pioneers, where he has served on the board for over fifteen years.

His public service includes appointments to the boards of One80 Place, the Gibbes Museum of Art, the Coastal Community Foundation, the Patriots Point Foundation, and the Berkeley-Charleston-Dorchester Council of Governments. From 2007 to 2009, he was a senior policy advisor to South Carolina Governor Mark Sanford.

Jack holds a BS in economics and an MBA, and his work reflects a deep integration of biblical character, sound judgment, and professional excellence. He has three grown children—Jack III, James, and Park—and three grandchildren. Since 2023, he and Jack III have co-written *Matter at Hand* Substack, exploring themes of faith, culture, and leadership.

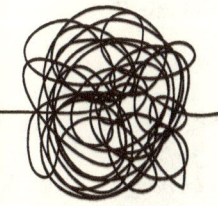

Endnotes

1   Søren Kierkegaard, *The Journals of Kierkegaard*, ed. Alexander Dru (New York: Harper & Brothers, 1959), 138.
2   John Henry Newman, *Selected Sermons* (New York: Paulist Press, 1994), 291.
3   Charles Taylor, *Sources of the Self*, (Cambridge, MA: Harvard University Press, 1989), 13.
4   Taylor, 13.
5   Rick Atkinson, *The Day of Battle: The War in Sicily and Italy, 1943-1944* (New York: Henry Holt & Company, 2008), 558–563.
6   A. W. Tozer, *The Pursuit of God*, (Camp Hill, PA: Christian Publications, Inc., 1982), 55.
7   Søren Kierkegaard, *The Journals of Kierkegaard*, ed. Alexander Dru (New York: Harper & Brothers, 1959), 138.
8   Simon Blackburn, *Mirror, Mirror: The Uses and Abuses of Self-Love* (Princeton: Princeton University Press, 2014), 174.
9   John Owen, *Sin and Temptation* (Portland, OR: Multnomah Press, 1983), 132.
10 J. B. Phillips, *The New Testament in Modern English*, rev. ed. (New York: Macmillan, 1972), 335.
11 Tozer, 9.
12 Tozer, 9.
13 J. Oswald Sanders, *Spiritual Leadership: Principles of Excellence for Every Believer*, rev. ed. (Chicago: Moody Press, 1981), 181.
14 Gordon MacDonald, *Restoring Your Spiritual Passion* (Nashville: Thomas Nelson Publishers, 1986), pp.64–9.

15 Søren Kierkegaard, *Purity of Heart Is to Will One Thing* (New York: Harper & Row Publishers, 1956), 189–90.

16 Kierkegaard, 191.

17 Jean-Luc Marion, *Prolegomena to Charity*, tr. Stephen E. Lewis (New York: Fordham University Press, 2002), 163.

18 Dallas Willard, *The Spirit of the Disciplines: Understanding How God Changes Lives* (San Francisco: HarperCollins Publishers, 1988), 160.

19 Willard, 160.

20 Phillips, 335.

21 Richard Foster, *The Celebration of Discipline* (San Francisco: Harper & Row Publishers, 1978), 95.

22 Brother Lawrence, *The Practice of the Presence of God* (Springdale, PA: Whitaker House, 1982), 67.

23 Henri Nouwen, *The Only Necessary Thing,* ed. Wendy Wilson Greer (New York: The Crossroad Publishing Company, 2014), 107.

24 Nouwen, 37.

25 Phillips, 135.

26 Quoted in Parker J. Palmer, *Let Your Life Speak* (San Francisco: Jossey-Bass, 2000), 16.

27 Charles Duhigg, *The Power of Habit: Why We Do What We Do in Life and Business* (New York: Random House, 2014).

28 Taylor, 13.

29 Reinhold Niebuhr, *Moral Man and Immoral Society* (Louisville, KY: Westminster John Knox Press, 2001), 275–6.

30 Taylor, 28.

31 Taylor, 13.

32 Taylor, 218.

33 Quoted in Tim Keller, *The Meaning of Marriage: Facing the Complexities of Commitment with the Wisdom of God* (New York: Dutton, 2011), 90.

34 Quoted in Keller, 94.

35 Cited in Jennifer Levitz, "More Young Adults Living with Parents than a Romantic Partner," *The Wall Street Journal*, May 24, 2016, https://www.wsj.com/articles/more-young-adults-living-with-parents-than-a-romantic-partner-1464098436.

36 Quoted Keller, 39.

37 Linda J. Waite and Maggie Gallagher, *The Case for Marriage: Why Married People Are Happier, Healthier, and Better Off Financially* (New York: Doubleday, 2000).

38 Waite, "5 Marriage Myths," pp. 20–21. This article was based on remarks delivered at Brigham Young University in November 2000, in which Dr. Waite summarized her findings in *The Case for Marriage.*

39 Waite, "5 Marriage Myths," p. 21.

40 Waite, "5 Marriage Myths," p. 21.

41 U.S. Department of Health and Human Services, Office of the Surgeon General. "Our Epidemic of Loneliness and Isolation: The U.S. Surgeon General's Advisory on the Healing Effects of Social Connection and Community" (Washington DC, 2023).

42 See Howard A. Snyder, *The Radical Wesley & Patterns for Church Renewal* (Grand Rapids: Zondervan, 1987).

43 Robert Greenleaf, *Servant Leadership* (Mahway, NJ: Paulist Press, 2002), 233.

44 Greenleaf, 62–63.

45 For a brilliant discussion of this, see Reinhold Niebuhr's *Moral Man and Immoral Society*, especially chapter 5, "The Ethical Attitudes of Privileged Classes." There is much in this chapter that speaks to economic structures that are no longer current, but Niebuhr frames clearly the distortions that privilege creates for our perspectives.

46 Newman, 291.